Endorsements

"*Soul Gardening* is creatively written to encourage and inspire no matter what season you are in. The open invitation to experience the heavenly Father's love from the 'gardener's' perspective was truly refreshing. Renee's painful personal experiences will plant hope within hearts—hope that beautiful things bloom planted in dark places."

—**Ashlee Mincer**, Author of *Life After Abortion: A Woman's Journey to Healing and God's Miracle Placed Within*

"In *Soul Gardening,* Renee Fisher invites the reader on a heartfelt journey through her own story of grief and hope. Renee elegantly encourages us to trust our spiritual seasons to the Lord of Hosts. I found such comfort and inspiration in knowing He alone can prepare me for what lies ahead. She encouraged me to boldly get curious about the beauty of my own garden. Renee is a master tour guide and a dream encourager."

—**Kim Roberts Mosko**, wife, mother, and daughter of Christ; Author of *Old Women Show Your Arms and Share Your Stories: Finding God's Persistent Presence in Everyday Life*

"Whether you are in a season of stagnation or in a season of flourishing, *Soul Gardening* is the perfect companion for your journey. Renee's greatest gift is coaching you to dream in all seasons of life. Words of encouragement, illustrations of beauty, and gentle nudging toward digging deeper are sprinkled throughout this amazing work of art. This book is one I will be reaching for time and time again."

—**Ronel Sidney**, Storyteller, and Author of *Freestyle Faith: Around the Table*

"Renee Fisher is a master at painting a picture that brings you on a journey of life's ups and downs. Throughout her own personal season, whether it be winter, spring, summer, or fall, she beckons us to hold on and trust the Lord until you see the seeds He has sown in the garden of your soul come to pass."

—**Maria Durso**, Speaker and Author of *Ageless: The Secret to the Spiritual Fountain of Youth*

"We live in a culture that only values one season—the harvest. This leaves the majority of us feeling like the other seasons we experience need a fast-forward button. Renee's words helped me understand for the very first time that God desires growth and purpose in every single season—not just the harvest. With Renee's soul-searching reflection questions, personal stories, and invitations for growth in every chapter, *Soul Gardening* is a game-changer for followers of Jesus pursuing dreams in a world that has forgotten the value of *every* season."

—**Rachel Lohman**, Founder, Hope Again Collective

"Renee Fisher's heart for gardens is not just a hobby she enjoys—it's become the theme of her life. In *Soul Gardening: Finding God in Every Season,* Renee not only shares how she found God in every season of her life, but how gardens are like dreams, ready to be planted, cultivated, grown, and harvested. Join Renee as she takes you on a beautiful tour through a spiritual garden of your own dreams, learn what it takes to see the seed of your dreams planted, tended to, and harvested, and how the creator of all gardens is present during each season from dream seed to the fruit."

—**Robin Grunder**, Author, Life-Story & Legacy Writer, Founder of Legacy Press

"I have been following the journey of *Soul Gardening: Finding God in Every Season* since it was just a seed in the heart and mind of the creative, talented, and caring author, Renee Fisher. Personally, my soul is nourished in a garden—and in the reading of this book, set in a garden. No matter what season of life you are in, the biblical truths, beauty, and bountiful life-transforming applications will help you grow and blossom."

—**Pam Farrel**, Author of 54 books including bestselling *Men Are Like Waffles, Women Are Like Spaghetti*, and the award-winning *Discovering the Bible: Creative Bible Study Experience* series

"Renee has created such a beautiful and inspiring guide to help anyone to understand the four seasons of life, fulfilling our given purpose and achieving our dreams. Her willingness both to walk the gardens with you and to share her own story leaves you feeling heard, understood, and encouraged. She reminds us to trust in God and hold on through the seasons, because you will harvest all that has been sown for you, and by you, exactly when He plans for you to bloom. Endless dreams are awaiting you in the gardens of your soul; just seek and trust in Him always."

—**Melissa Morse**, Author of *Never Give Up: A Father's Pursuit of His Child's Heart*

"Soul Gardening is so eye-opening and encouraging! Renee has brought to light the different seasons of our gardens. She walks us through each season with her own testimony and thought-provoking questions to cultivate thoughts of our own seasons. Through each season, we are reminded how to trust the Lord. Thank you, Renee, for letting the Lord speak through you on the pages of this book."

—**Angela McBride**, Author of *Ella's Story: One Family's Journey to Discovering Miracles Do Happen*

"In *Soul Gardening*, Renee taught me how to discern the seasons of my dreams. She not only shares her own stories of soul gardening with vulnerability and confession, but also comes alongside you to intentionally reflect on your own. I found myself looking back on my old dreams previously manifest with the ability to name the seasons of their memorable hardships and joys. This filled me with wisdom and encouragement to faithfully farm for the fruition of more! Renee taught me that even though each season comes with a unique pest, theme, and miracle, I can count on God's presence and peace in every season. She ends with an invitation to continue your soul gardening in the most beautiful of ways, and I realized then how many seeds she had planted in me, with scriptures rich on every page and many watered right then and there with tears falling down my face!"

—**Amy Burgin**, Southwest Research Institute Sr. Computer Scientist for NASA and Christgazing Podcast Co-Host

"As a novice gardener, I understand the wisdom gained when you get on your knees, put your hands in the dirt, and plant things. Renee beautifully uses gardening and the changing seasons to teach us about living the best life God desires for all His children. Renee is a masterful storyteller and bravely weaves the story of her sometimes heartbreaking and sometimes joyful story together with God's truth and His promises to help you find your spiritual season. If you dream, let Renee take you on a stroll through your soul garden."

—**Tamela Turbeville**, Author of *A Rescued Life: A Story of Secrets and Shame, Hope and Healing*

SOUL
GARDENING

FINDING GOD IN
EVERY SEASON

Renee Fisher

Copyright © 2022 by Renee Fisher
ReneeFisher.com

Published by Renee Fisher & Co. LLC
102 E Kimberly Rd Ste I #107
Davenport, IA 52806

Unless otherwise identified, all Scripture quotations in this publication are taken from The Holy Bible, English Standard Version. ESV® Text Edition: 2016. Copyright © 2001 by Crossway Bibles, a publishing ministry of Good News Publishers.

Scripture taken from the New King James Version® (NKJV). Copyright © 1982 by Thomas Nelson. Used by permission. All rights reserved.

Scripture taken from the *Holy Bible*, New Living Translation (NLT), copyright © 1996, 2004, 2015 by Tyndale House Foundation. Used by permission of Tyndale House Publishers, Inc., Carol Stream, Illinois 60188. All rights reserved.

Scripture taken from the New American Standard Bible® (NASB), Copyright © 1960, 1971, 1977, 1995, 2020 by The Lockman Foundation. All rights reserved.

Scripture taken from the King James Version (KJV), is public domain.

Cover & Interior Layout Design: © Nelly Murariu at PixBeeDesign.com
All book interior photos Copyright © Renee Fisher

ISBN Paperback: 978-1-7337490-2-2
ISBN eBook: 978-1-7337490-3-9
Library of Congress Control Number: 2021911398

Dedication

To the LORD of hosts ~ the best garden tour guide ever.
Thank You for finding me!

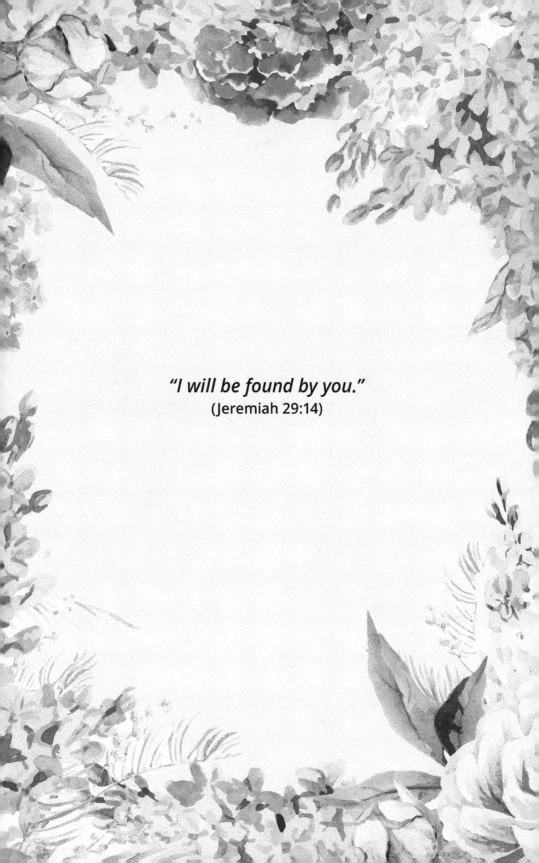

"I will be found by you."
(Jeremiah 29:14)

Contents

Letter to the Reader

> "The concept of paradise and God's presence can be traced from Genesis 3 to Ezekiel 47 and ultimately to Revelation 21-22.
> The entire Word of God is a story of how we lost a garden and God's process to bring us back into his presence in a garden." (1)

Life began in a garden. The garden is where humans were created with unfiltered access to God. I believe the best place to find God is still in the garden, no matter the season. The

Life began in a garden.

good news is that you don't even have to look far. Whether you are searching for God in your own backyard, walking laps at a local park, or enjoying a stroll in a botanical garden— He is with you. His Indwelling Presence is *in* you, filling you to live the abundant life (see Romans 8:9; Ephesians 2:22; John 10:10).

I'm on a quest to find God in *every* season. And it wouldn't be possible if Jesus Himself hadn't been sent by the Father to go on a quest to reconcile us back to Him.

This.

This is why I wrote *Soul Gardening*. To help us see this open invitation from Jesus, the gardener, to all who search for Him. In fact, you don't even have to be into gardening. Look at Mary, the first person to search for Jesus after His resurrection. She went to the garden tomb because she was desperate to find His body and anoint Him. Instead, she found Jesus sitting there waiting for her. He found her, and she didn't even recognize Him. She thought he was the gardener.

"And of course he was—he is—the gardener! This was the dawn of the new creation. The Gardener was up at the crack of dawn doing the work the first Adam failed to do—extending the boundaries of paradise into the wilderness of this world." (2)

In Soul Gardening, *I hope you discover Jesus in your soul garden and allow Him to find you.*

In *Soul Gardening*, I hope you discover Jesus in your soul garden and allow Him to find you. Like Mary, when you desperately search for Jesus, you will discover that He was waiting for you all along. Doesn't that excite you? Even in your darkest hour, He is waiting for you! It is my prayer that you find Him through the pages of this book. I pray also that my story helps you find God in your story. Jeremiah 29:14 says, "'I will be found by you,' declares the Lord."

No matter which season you're currently in, God can be found by you.

❖ **Winter:** Your dreams are...*waiting for the right time.*

❖ **Spring:** Your dreams are...*preparing to sprout.*

❖ **Summer:** Your dreams are...*ready to harvest.*

❖ **Fall:** Your dreams are...*treasured in your storehouse.*

Join me on a sacred journey
to learn how to dream in
a garden, discover your
spiritual season, and find
peace for your soul.

Is this something you desire? To find God in *every* season? If you find yourself nodding your head in agreement, experiencing a tingle in your heart or goosebumps on your arms—then I hope you'll come along. Join me on a sacred journey to learn how to dream in a garden, discover your spiritual season, and find peace for your soul. Because life gets stuck sometimes. Maybe you don't like your job or relationship status (or lack of one). Maybe you're waiting on God for children. Maybe the place where you're currently living doesn't feel like home. Maybe your health isn't the greatest. I just described my life from four difficult seasons.

Friend, don't let your life circumstances or season define your happiness. Your joy comes from God. You can dream where you are planted. You can go on a quest to heal your soul in the cool of the garden with the Lord of hosts.

What about you? I don't know what you're going through, or why you feel stuck—but I do know that you and I need help to grow. I also want you to know that you don't need to wait to search for God until life becomes difficult. Speaking from personal experience, I tend to seek Him less when life is flourishing. It's usually in a winter season when I am more likely to search for God. It's easy to let unmet longings fester and cause bitterness to spring up and block the path to finding God in difficult seasons.

Friend, don't let your life circumstances or season define your happiness. Your joy comes from God. You can dream where you are planted. You can go on a quest to heal your soul in the cool of the garden with the Lord of hosts.

I hope you'll give me the honor of being your garden tour guide. Please flip over a page with me to the Introduction where you'll find a garden party invitation with your name on it! I saved a seat for you.

Your Dream Defender,

Renee Fisher

Introduction
Garden Party Invitation

"The future belongs to those who believe
in the beauty of their dreams." (1)

Welcome to the garden, dear reader. Please join me for a garden party. I've saved a seat for you on the bench starting...*now.*

Benches are one of my favorite things about gardens. At the time of publishing this book, I've visited forty-two gardens in fifteen states and two countries. I've enjoyed taking pictures of the various benches I've spotted in gardens from Hawaii to London. What I love most about benches is that they offer a space to sit, breathe, and listen to nature. (If you would like to see the photo galleries from each garden I've visited, please visit my personal website PeacefulFisher.com).

Let's go ahead and practice sitting on a bench in nature. Close your eyes and take three deep breaths. I hope that helps calm your mind to get you excited to meet with God throughout the pages of this book. I've had some of my most intimate conversations with God on the benches of city parks, gardens, and in my own backyard. It is my hope that you will take this book to your favorite chair or bench and sit outside for a while. Please don't feel rushed to read through *Soul Gardening.* Each chapter is meant to help you slow down and savor the season, as well tend to your own soul garden. As you read, you'll work through these seven principles to help you grow slow:

1. Every Garden Starts with Good Soil

2. Each Dream is a Seed Waiting to Be Planted

3. Each Seed is Planted in the Dark

4. You Cannot Sow and Harvest in the Same Season

5. Ripe Fruit Bruises Easily

6. The Harvest is the Word of God

7. After Each Harvest...Rest

At the *Soul Gardening* Garden Party, please BYOGT—bring your own gardening tools—as this will help you take advantage of the questions found at the end of each chapter. I recommend grabbing your Bible, colored pens, and a journal before you get started. Also, a garden party wouldn't be fun without interactive games, so you'll find some in the back of the book. You can do them yourself or with friends. While you read and journal, feel free to listen to the playlist I created of all the songs listed in the book at bit.ly/SoulGardening.

As you read *Soul Gardening*, I'd love it if you would RSVP to me at Renee@ReneeFisher.com and let me know that you are coming to the garden party so I can encourage you along the journey. As a bonus, I want you to know that your garden invitation is also good for the garden parties I host online through my professional website, ReneeFisher.com. Once I am able, I will begin hosting garden parties in person at a garden near you (my REALLY big dream)!

Without further ado, it is with great joy to welcome you to dream in a garden, discover your spiritual season, and find peace.

Let nature nurture your soul.
Let's dream together
while learning from the
rhythms of the seasons.

SECTION I

Dream in a Garden

CHAPTER 1

Every Garden Starts with Good Soil

"For us to function well, our souls need nourishment. Our souls are what I like to think of as the spiritual side of us." (1)

I am thrilled to be your tour guide! I can't wait to show you that you don't even have to like gardening—or have two green thumbs—to get the most out of this book. (I confess that I didn't learn how to keep my houseplants alive until I was thirty-five.) Before you get started, please flip back a few pages and make sure you've read the Letter to the Reader and Introduction, which includes a garden party invitation.

As mentioned in the invitation, you'll need a couple of tools to get started, including your Bible, colored pens, and a journal to get the most out of the questions at the end of each chapter. I also strongly recommend a few more useful *Soul Gardening* tools that you can use to grow. Every tool is given by God to be used to cultivate the soil of your soul, which is the foundation for all growth. This list is not meant to be exhaustive.

Every tool is given by God to be used to cultivate the soil of your soul, which is the foundation for all growth.

Please feel free to add tools to the list below and identify what each one cultivates for you:

- ⚙ **Prayer:** Cultivates...listening, talking to, and conversing with God

- ⚙ **Reading the Bible:** Cultivates...hearing and doing the Word of God

- ⚙ **Bible Study:** Cultivates...a deeper knowledge of God and His Word

- ⚙ **Meditating:** Cultivates...being mindful of God and staying present with Him

- ⚙ **Journaling:** Cultivates...writing down important thoughts, feelings, quotes, prayers, and anything you want to remember

- ⚙ **Worship:** Cultivates...bringing God praise, honor, and glory, as well as a soft heart

- ⚙ **Hearing the Holy Spirit:** Cultivates...rest and peace to hear God's gentle whispers

- ⚙ **Christian Books, Blogs, Social Media Posts, and Podcasts:** Cultivate...different perspectives and diversity of thoughts to challenge growth

- ⚙ **Wise Counsel:** Cultivates...making important or difficult decisions easier, as well as accountability and submission

- ⚙ **One-Day or Weekend Retreats:** Cultivate...a place and time free of distractions to grow spiritually

❀ _____: Cultivates... _____

❀ _____: Cultivates... _____

❀ _____: Cultivates... _____

The good news is that when you use one of these tools, you are cultivating your relationship with God so that you can always tend your soul garden. The more you tend

Always tend your soul garden.

to your relationship with God, the easier it is to find Him in *every* season. And that's not even the best part!

"All of this leads up to the most important aspect of God's art, and one that concerns us personally: 'And God said, Let us make man in our image, after our likeness: ... So God created man in his own image, in the image of God created he him...'" (2)

God is the first landscape architect. He didn't just *plant* the garden of Eden and stop there! He created man and woman *in His image*. You and I were both planted and planned by God to do good works before we were born.

You and I were both planted and planned by God to do good works before we were born.

❀ Psalm 139:13-14 says, "For you formed my inward parts; you knitted me together in my mother's womb. I praise you, for I am fearfully and wonderfully made. Wonderful are your works; my soul knows it very well."

⊛ Ephesians 2:10 says, "For we are his workmanship, created in Christ Jesus for good works, which God prepared beforehand, that we should walk in them."

You and I are created in His image. I don't know about you, but the more I spend time in nature discovering new flowers and plants, the more I see God's fingerprints of beauty in the vibrant varieties He created, like you and me. Thanks to God's redemptive work in the Garden of Gethsemane and triumph over the grave, you and I both have the pleasure of knowing our immense worth, which gives us the confidence to find God in the garden. Have you ever seen an ugly flower? I know I haven't. That is because God doesn't create ugly. And if you do see one, it's probably because of bad weather or owner neglect. His creation is good and beautiful because He created it.

God wants you to create, dream up, and tend to your own soul garden, because He wants to shine His beauty through your life. As a Certified Christian Life Coach, I've had the pleasure of coaching clients ranging in ages from seventeen to eighty-seven! Each client reveals God's beauty through their life and how they see the world. Just as

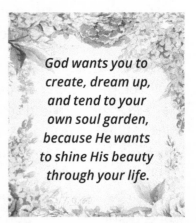

God wants you to create, dream up, and tend to your own soul garden, because He wants to shine His beauty through your life.

a flower doesn't worry about competing with the next one—it just blooms—whatever gifts or skills you have, even if they seem hidden in seed form, are dreams ready to be planted by

God. (More on this in Chapter 2). As you read through this book, I hope you bloom, friend!

The Good Soil

Every gardener knows to start with good soil that will nourish the seeds planted. It's the same physically and spiritually. Every garden starts with good soil. This is the first spiritual principle. It is important to have the right soil so that whatever seeds you plant in faith can—and will—harvest God-sized dreams for the future. You'll read more in the next chapter, but first, let's go ahead and define what "good soil" means from a spiritual perspective. Mark 4:3-8 says,

> "'Listen! Behold, a sower went out to sow. And as he sowed, some seed fell along the path, and the birds came and devoured it. Other seed fell on rocky ground, where it did not have much soil, and immediately it sprang up, since it had no depth of soil. And when the sun rose, it was scorched, and since it had no root, it withered away. Other seed fell among thorns, and the thorns grew up and choked it, and it yielded no grain. And other seeds fell into good soil and produced grain, growing up and increasing and yielding thirtyfold and sixtyfold and a hundredfold.'"

It's interesting that the crowds didn't press Jesus further on the meaning. It wasn't until Jesus was alone with His disciples that He revealed the spiritual significance to them. Mark 4:20 records Jesus's response. He said, "'But those that were sown on the good soil are the ones who hear the word and accept it and bear fruit, thirtyfold and sixtyfold and a hundredfold.'" You know what this means? The good soil is *you*!

Every garden starts
with good soil. This is the
first spiritual principle.

You are the soul who hears the Word, accepts it, and bears fruit for His kingdom.

The good soil is you! You are the soul who hears the Word, accepts it, and bears fruit for His kingdom.

Friend, how do you cultivate the good soil of your soul? How do you know if your soul is growing and being nourished? First, let's talk about those things that hinder or ruin soul growth. They are:

- ❀ Devouring birds

- ❀ Lack of depth

- ❀ Too much heat

- ❀ Choking thorns

What joy stealers, depth distractions, hot button triggers, or restrictive means keep you from hearing, accepting, and bearing fruit in your soul garden? Before you answer that question, I want to encourage you with this thought: God wants to meet

God wants to meet with you personally and speak directly to the very thing that threatens to keep you from Him.

with you personally and speak directly to the very thing that threatens to keep you from Him.

Notice what God first asked Eve in the garden after she disobeyed. "He said, 'Who told you that you were naked?'" (Genesis 3:11a). God didn't beat around the bush...er, fig leaf she used to hide her shame. He cut straight to Eve's deceived heart. For me, it was the question, "Who told you that you can't have kids?" When God asked me this question, my fig leaf walls crumbled. I wonder what God would ask you. Maybe He'd say, "Who told you that you are...?" or "Who told you that you can't...?"

If you're struggling to give God access to the good soil of your soul, I hope you'll find comfort in God's redemption plan that began in the garden. Let me ask you this: Do you desire to have God speak to you personally no matter where you are, or what season you currently find yourself in? I hope you said, "Yes!" The garden is where your redemption began as creatures made in His image to work, rest, and enjoy His presence.

> *The garden is where your redemption began as creatures made in His image to work, rest, and enjoy His presence.*

> "We often talk about our desires for the future as the restoration of Eden or returning to Eden. But the reality is, the Eden we read about in Genesis 1 and 2 wasn't yet everything God intended for his creation. It was unsullied but incomplete. It was bursting with potential, but it wasn't yet all that God intended for the home he should share with his people. From the very beginning Eden was not meant to be static; it was headed somewhere. Likewise, Adam and Eve were not yet all that God intended for his people to be. They were sinless but not yet glorious, at least not as glorious as God intended them to become." (3)

"Headed somewhere." "Not all they were intended to be yet." Two profound thoughts. I am always afraid my story isn't headed anywhere or that my life won't have any impact for the kingdom of God. You and I are both waiting on a new heaven and earth, including glorified bodies that will be *even better than Eden. Glory be!* This is good news. I don't know about you, but I am ready for this quest. I'm pack-ing my bags—spiritually speaking—and I'm excited for the adventure. What about you?

You and I are both waiting on a new heaven and earth, including glorified bodies that will be even better than Eden.

Are you ready to find God in the garden of your soul and experience His presence? Like right now? I can't wait for this future redemption of the new heaven and earth that Revelation 21-22 speaks of—not to mention our glorified bodies. But, until this day comes, you and I can continue the adventure between the "already" and the "not yet." What a glorious thought! This is the best kind of direction.

I don't know about you, but no amount of progress in my own life ever seems to be deep enough to grow the kind of fruit that satisfies. The same can also be said for a physical garden. There is always more work to be done. Do you know what I mean?

"God is, even now, working out his plan to do far more than simply restore his creation to the state of integrity that was Eden. Christ came to accomplish what was necessary to open the way for us, not just back into the garden of Eden, but into a home that will be even better than Eden and a life that will be even better than the life Adam and Eve enjoyed there." (4)

My Story

I want to share my story with you of how I became a dreamer. Grab some coffee or tea and maybe a Kleenex or two because my story is messy and certainly not pretty. It started at the tender age of eleven. My parents left for an overseas trip when I was in the fifth grade. Something inside of me broke that day. God knew *that* day was coming because He answered my first-ever major prayer request the very instant I waved a tearful goodbye with my brother and our adopted grandma by my side.

I looked up and spotted the most beautiful orange tabby cat. I quickly called him down off the roof. He stayed by my side the entire time my parents were gone. My brother, Richard, named him Lemon. When they returned, they let me keep him—even though my dad didn't like cats. (It took many counselors over the years to help me see I was being brave. Even on my darkest day, God gave me the courage to call the cat down off the roof and make him mine.)

I couldn't stop crying for weeks after my parents returned. My mom took me to various medical doctors—all of whom couldn't find anything wrong with me. I was always starving, shaking, or paralyzed with fear to leave the house. My parents helped me find a breakthrough through a new study by Dr. Neil T. Anderson entitled *7 Steps to Freedom in Christ*. They found a couple who walked me through each step, to confess my sins and allow God to help me with every one of my fears. This process of confessing each lie and replacing it with a Bible verse is how I learned to take my thoughts captive.

Here is a Bible verse and a wonderful quote to illustrate this point:

⊛ 2 Corinthians 10:5 (NKJV) says, "Casting down arguments and every high thing that exalts itself against the knowledge of God, bringing every thought into captivity to the obedience of Christ."

⊛ "Every time I give in to a fearful thought, I am taking a bite from the fruit of the tree of knowledge of good and evil all over again." (5)

I learned that every fear I had could be traced back to a lie I believed to be true. Maybe the same can be said for you. It took me many years to learn how to eradicate the lies I believed and which truths from the Bible I needed to pray through and cultivate.

I learned that every fear I had could be traced back to a lie I believed to be true. Maybe the same can be said for you.

I still have Dr. Anderson's orange booklet today. It's one of the things I'll always keep from my childhood. For a time, this kind of prayer helped me manage my anxiety before the nurse practitioner in my twenties diagnosed me with Generalized Anxiety Disorder (GAD) and prescribed an anti-anxiety medication that I still take daily.

Prayer helped me to find God as a child. God knew I would need this because as a freshman in high school, I started having more health problems. I got my first-ever ingrown toenail that I didn't think was a big deal. I had no idea I was suddenly allergic to Band-Aids, and I broke out with itchy white bumps all over my toe. Since I had never had a rash before, I scratched them without thinking—until they oozed. The rash (eczema) spread so fast that it took the skin off both of my feet. I had to wrap my feet in sterile gauze bandages and stretch socks over them. They barely fit into my Birkenstocks. Any time I had to change my bandages, they ripped off any new flesh that started growing and made them raw, itchy, and oozy all over again.

At the same time, there was this boy...

When my first teenage relationship didn't work out, I was crushed. I cried even harder than when my parents left on their trip. Only this time, my years of confessing lies and replacing them with truth from the Bible kicked in. Even though I ignored it, I knew *why* I was crying. I was believing the lie that no boy would ever love me again!

My rash ended up spreading from my feet to my face from the tears I cried. I was admitted to Children's Hospital in San Diego, California. I couldn't open my eyes. I looked like a burn victim. My feet and face itched and burned like hell. If anything came in contact with them, including the faintest breeze—I was sent into shock. In the hospital, my mom read Hosea 6:1-3 (NLT) to me.

> "Come, let us return to the Lord. He has torn us to pieces; now he will heal us. He has injured us; now he will bandage our wounds. In just a short time he will restore us, so that we may live in his presence. Oh, that we might know the Lord! Let us press on to know him. He will respond to us as surely as the arrival of dawn or the coming of rains in early spring."

My mom shared with me that if God allowed me to be torn into pieces, then He could also bandage my wounds. I knew right then in the hospital that my prayer life wasn't enough. I needed to read the Word for myself! I didn't want to rely on my mom's faith. I wanted my own promise from God. I couldn't believe my mom found a verse in the Bible just for me and my situation, which is why I asked my parents for Christmas that year if I could have the same *NLT One Year Bible* my mom read to me in the hospital. After they got it for me, I made a vow to read through the entire Bible. I was desperate to find a promise from God for my healing. Sure enough, I found it before the year was up!

> 1 Peter 5:10 (NLT) says, "In his kindness God called you to share in his eternal glory by means of Christ Jesus. So after you have suffered a little while, he will restore, support, and strengthen you, and he will place you on a firm foundation."

A "little while" turned into many years of learning how to walk in God's healing. Through it all, I never stopped reading the Bible and journaling. I didn't know it at the time, but God was preparing me to become an author to share my story to the hurting and broken. He was teaching me how to forgive myself when life didn't turn out as I expected.

I thought I was going to become a high school math teacher, yet God allowed me to suffer through severe anxiety and fast-spreading eczema so that He could call me into ministry to encourage those who also suffered. That year reading through the Bible for the first time, God didn't just give me a promise of healing in 1 Peter 5:10, but He also promised me a husband in Isaiah 34:16 (NKJV):

> "Search from the book of the Lord, and read:
> Not one of these shall fail;
> Not one shall lack her mate.
> For My mouth has commanded it, and His Spirit has *gathered* them." (emphasis mine)

It was during the editing process of writing my second book, *Not Another Dating Book,* that God brought Marc to the same doorstep where my brother and I found Lemon the cat. I was co-hosting a singles' growth group for twenty-somethings through my church. Marc signed up, came to my house, and it was love at first sight. I was single twelve years, ten months, and twenty-four days from the day God promised me a husband to the day Marc proposed on Coronado Beach, California. I didn't just find one promise from God that first year but two as I was reading through the *One Year Bible*.

God *gathered* Marc and I while using North Coast Church's twenty-something growth groups and my parents' house to facilitate our meeting. I'll stop there for now. There's so much more to my story than just living *happily ever after,* but I'll wait to share that with you in future chapters.

Your Story

It wasn't until my twenties that I became a dreamer. I have a mentor to thank for this! She asked me the question, "Renee, the Holy Spirit wants to know—if you were well what would you do?" That question lit a fire in my heart. I began writing down a list of all the things I could think of that I wanted to do with my life if health issues weren't in the way. After I showed my mentor the list, we met intentionally to discuss what it could look like to sow these dreams. If it weren't for her guidance, I don't know where I would be today.

If I were to ask you to write down all the things you want to do with your life regardless of your circumstances, I wonder what would be on your list. I'd also love to hear *your* story. This is one of the perks about being a Life Coach. I have the pleasure of hearing stories from dreamers like you. I also love asking questions like:

⊛   What are your hopes for the future?

⊛   What are you currently struggling with?

Maybe you're unsure of how to find God in your specific situation. I had to write down each dream in order to see which ones God wanted me to sow first so that He could harvest later. I'm grateful that God answered many of the dreams on that list. This is also what I wish for you.

Remember the two questions I asked at the beginning of the chapter? How do you cultivate the good soil of your soul? How do you know if your soul is growing and being nourished? Praying and reading the Bible are the two main ways I have cultivated the soil of my soul. If those aren't your favorite tools, please refer to the list at the beginning of the chapter. Journaling is my favorite way of nourishing and monitoring soul growth. What about you?

I wonder if there are any lies that stand in your way of receiving God's restoration and enjoying His presence so that you can grow deeper in Him? Are you ready to cultivate the good soil of your soul, get your hands dirty

Be willing to cultivate the good soil of your soul because Your Father, the Gardner, cares about you and wants to spend eternity with you in paradise.

and get to work to meet with God in the garden? I hope you are because a garden paradise awaits! Be willing to cultivate the good soil of your soul because Your Father, the Gardner, cares about you and wants to spend eternity with you in paradise.

In the rest of the book, you're going to put the gardening tools to good use and discover how to plant seeds, tend, and harvest your own soul garden. But first, let me pray for you:

Dear Dream-Giver Jesus,

Thank You for reminding me that You never leave me or forsake me. Help me stop hiding behind fig leaves. I want You to cut to the heart of my deception. Show me the lies I have been believing. Show me which seeds from the Word of God to plant in my heart so that I can grow in truth and grace. Help me to see myself as You see me—created in Your image. Open my ears to hear, hands to accept, and the soil of my soul to bear fruit. Grant me success on this soul gardening journey, I pray. Amen.

Soul Gardening **Questions for Further Reflection**

1. What is your favorite physical and/or spiritual gardening tools? Why?

    _____

    _____

    _____

    _____

    _____

    _____

    _____

2. Have you ever thought of yourself as "good soil?" What is the condition of your soul currently? Is it currently being nourished or does it feel complacent? Why?

_____

_____

_____

_____

_____

_____

_____

_____

3. Have you ever attached a Bible verse to your life whether for trials or dreams? Why or why not?

_____

_____

_____

_____

_____

_____

_____

_____

_____

_____

4. Are you currently experiencing any joy stealers, depth distractions, hot button triggers, or restrictive means that threaten to keep you from hearing, accepting, and bearing fruit in your soul garden? Take a few minutes through prayer and reflection to cultivate the soil of your soul. Then, confess each lie before God. Use the spaces below if you feel comfortable or write them in your own journal. Ask God which verses you can use in the Bible to replace the lies with the truth of His Word.

_____

_____

_____

_____

_____

_____

_____

_____

_____

_____

_____

_____

_____

_____

_____

_____

_____

CHAPTER 2

Each Dream is a Seed Waiting to be Planted

"To plant a garden is to believe in tomorrow." (1)

A seed planted is not hidden. In Matthew 25, there is a man with one talent who was afraid of his master. Instead of planting his talent in the ground, he hid it in the ground. *Wait.* Aren't these two the same thing? At first glance, *yes.* Digging a spot in the ground is the same thing as hiding something in the ground, but that's where it stops. The farmer knows that the seed must *die* in the ground to yield a harvest.

A seed planted is not hidden.

He immediately relinquishes his right to the seeds he plants by cultivating the soil so that the conditions for dying are best. In fact, he doesn't even have to pray about it. He just plants, waters, and waits for nature to do its thing. *Wow!*

Planting a seed in the ground is not just a physical action but a spiritual principle as well. Every seed needs to die before it sprouts. (We'll uncover more of what this means in Chapters 3 and 4.) If I'm not careful, my need for approval will cause me to be afraid of Jesus when He asks me to let go of my deepest desires, dreams, and talents so that He can bury them in the ground.

To die.

I wonder if you're like me, friend—instead of surrendering your seed dreams to God, you bury them yourself. Sometimes it seems easier to hide the dream away in fear. Then, after shame kicks in, you *hide* when you know God is tapping you on the shoulder to release your hands so He can plant the seed in the ground, water it, and watch it grow.

Is it okay that I've been calling you *friend*? I hope so. As children of God—He calls us His "friend" (John 15:15). I may have become a friend of God at the ripe young age of five, but—like I shared in Chapter 1—I didn't become a dreamer until my twenties. I allowed fear to cripple my dreams for two decades. I wonder if Jesus was ever afraid.

"Was Jesus afraid of doing the Father's will?" I think the answer is yes and no. He prayed in the Garden of Gethsemane with drops of sweat pouring out of His face like blood. He asked the Father three times to take it away, but ultimately—He obeyed. He was not afraid but knew the kind of gruesome suffering and torture that awaited Him. "'Not My will, but Yours, be done,'" He said (Luke 22:42).

Forgiveness is not the end of your story—or mine. After death comes life!

After Jesus was crucified, the stone was rolled shut, and everyone believed death had won. However, victory came three days later!!! Hallelujah! Now every physical *and* spiritual seed planted doesn't end in death. Forgiveness is not the end of your story—or mine. After death comes life!

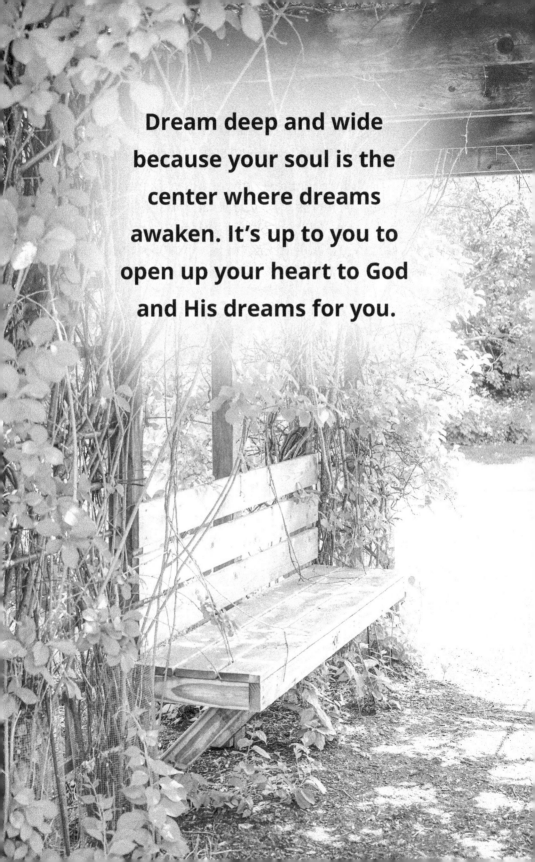

Dream deep and wide because your soul is the center where dreams awaken. It's up to you to open up your heart to God and His dreams for you.

"The future is given to those who are experienced
in groaning. The future is denied to those who have
been cynical and calloused and self-deceiving..." (2)

Maybe that's how you feel right now too, friend. Cynical.
Calloused. Self-deceived. Are you willing to let God speak
into the deep places of your soul? The places you can't let go
of due to fear, betrayal, and lost hope? And what about the
small crevices you think He doesn't care about?

He does!

Dream deep and wide because your soul is the center
where dreams awaken. It's up to you to open up your heart
to God and His dreams for you.

To Dream is to Live

Give yourself permission to dream. If you are currently
struggling to believe that God cares about *all* your dreams—
not just the spiritual kind—you are not alone. Remember,

*Give yourself
permission to
dream.*

nature is the slowest form of
art. It takes time to sit and soak
up God's presence. It takes
time to discover the beauty
that dances all around in the
ripple of rivers, the sass of a
sunset, and the fluorescent
flowers that bloom. This is true both physically and spiritually. If you're not sure which seeds to plant or are feeling
frustrated that the seeds you planted weeks, months, or
even years earlier are not showing fruit, you are also not
alone.

It's okay to dream slow. Nature doesn't rush and neither
should you. It's like this. If you plant one seed in the ground,

for instance, a flowering plant or vegetable of some kind, you harvest more than one flower or vegetable. This same principle applies to us spiritually as well. When you plant just *one* seed in the ground, God takes that seed and grows it into a beautiful masterpiece for a kingdom-sized harvest to impact those around you (see Ephesians 2:10). Your life is that seed, friend.

It's okay to dream slow. Nature doesn't rush and neither should you.

Let's go back even further. Before God created you, He already had a dream in mind. Jeremiah 1:5 says, "'Before I formed you in the womb I knew you, and before you were born I consecrated you; I appointed you a prophet to the nations.'" It is my prayer to dream you to life because you *are* a beautiful masterpiece. God has plans for you that He appointed before the world began. So how do you dream to live? The answer is found in Deuteronomy 13. Let's read.

> "If a prophet or a *dreamer of dreams* arises among you and gives you a sign or a wonder, and the sign or wonder that he tells you comes to pass, and if he says, 'Let us go after other gods,' which you have not known, 'and let us serve them,' you shall not listen to the words of that prophet or that dreamer of dreams. For the Lord your God is testing you, to know whether you love the Lord your God with all your heart and with all your soul." (Deuteronomy 13:1-3, *emphasis added*).

The Hebrew word **"dreamer of dreams"** is *chalam*, which means "to dream, to be healthy, strong and to restore to health." (3) Can you believe that one of the meanings of "dreamer of dreams" literally means "to restore to health"?

The moment I decided to
let go of the pain of my
past, I found healing for
the present and a pile of
dreams for my future.
God *still* had plans for me.
I hope you believe this, too.

If I hadn't looked up the meaning of "dreamer of dreams" in the Interlinear Bible, I wouldn't have found the twenty-four other verses that mention that same Hebrew word, including the only one that references the meaning "to restore to health," which is Isaiah 38:16:

> "O Lord, by these things men live, and in all these is the life of my spirit. Oh restore me to health and make me live!"

Putting Deuteronomy 13:1 and Isaiah 38:16 together, you read that being a "dreamer of dreams" can "restore to health" and "by these things men live." Isn't that incredible? To dream is to live! I know this to be true because God restored my health not once, not twice, but many times.

To dream is to live!

I shared in Chapter 1 the question a mentor asked me, "Renee, the Holy Spirit wants to know—if you were well what would you do?" It was the Holy Spirit inside of her that spoke to my soul, awakening the "dreamer of dreams" in me. She helped dream me to life. I pray I am a catalyst God uses to dream you to life also. The moment I decided to let go of the pain of my past, I found healing for the present and a pile of dreams for my future. God *still* had plans for me. I hope you believe this, too. I firmly believe that you cannot miss your spiritual season (more on this in Section II).

Our dreams are important to Him. I don't know about you, but there have definitely been a few times when I have felt like I was at the point of dying, whether it was from heartbreak, anxiety, or rashes over my physical body. Like Hezekiah, I asked the Lord to hear my prayer and restore me to health and life. Are you longing for new life, or is there someone God is leading you to help dream to life? Maybe that

Our dreams are important to Him.

seed you're afraid to plant will not only help restore you but others to health and life.

Did you know there is price tag to every dream? The front side shows how much *you're* going to pay to plant the seed, die to the dream, and trust God with the harvest. The back side shows the price *others* will pay if you don't! *Wow!* I heard this metaphor from Janine Mason at the Dream Culture Conference at Bethel Church in Redding, California. I don't remember the exact words, but the concept stayed with me, and I hope it stays with you, too! It can be so easy to give up when life gets hard, but don't quit dreaming because others are counting on you. *Literally.*

My Story

My number one dream as a young girl was to travel to New York City. I have to thank Marc for suggesting we visit the New York Botanical Garden on our first trip there. We were looking for fun things to do in each of the five boroughs after Marc's work conference to celebrate my birthday together. We took the subway from Manhattan to the Bronx to visit the garden. After we got off, we walked for what felt like forever. I remember yelling at Marc that we were *never* going to find the entrance to the garden. He encouraged me to keep walking instead of responding to my *hangry* protests! Besides hunger, the summer heat made me want to turn around and go back. I was ready to give up when we finally found the entrance to the garden. (I need to get one of those shirts that says, "I'm sorry for the things I said when I was hungry" and wear it every time we travel!)

Marc *immediately* bought me an ice-cold drink in the NYBG cafe, and over the next hour we *oohed* and *awed* over its lush wide and open spaces. The New York Botanical Garden was green and grand. There were indoor and outdoor gardens with all sorts of unique plants. Some gardens were cultivated and others were wild. There were beautiful fountains and natural streams of water. And the trees! Oh my! They were humungous, and so many. The garden made us forget we were in one of the busiest and loudest cities in the world.

Since my first visit to the New York Botanical Garden in 2014, my eyes were opened to the beauty of nature. It was then I understood, "There are always flowers for those who want to see them" (4) But I have a confession to make. It took me over two years to connect dreaming with gardens. That is because Marc and I felt stuck. We were newlyweds living in Southern California, and we were house poor. He felt stuck in his job, and I felt stuck with my publishing career. We also struggled to find church community. Instead of thanking God that we owned a home in Southern California, Marc's job was stable, and my dreams of becoming an author had come true—we complained. We believed we were stuck and focused on what we *didn't* have. (Have you ever been there?)

There are always flowers for those who want to see them

When I married Marc at the age of twenty-nine, I knew he did *not* want to stay in California permanently. A few years after we got married, he found a number of software engineer job openings in Austin, Texas. His current company didn't want him to quit, so they gave him the opportunity to work remotely so we could move when we were ready, which we did one year later. As an author, I could move any-where, but unbeknownst to Marc—before we ever met—I had made a vow to never move *back* to Texas! That's right. Back.

I had briefly lived in Texas as a single twenty-something as part of a discipleship training program to become an overseas missionary. A few months after living in Texas, my eczema returned with a fury, and I lost the skin off my hands. I had to return home and wasn't able to complete the program or go overseas with my team to India. I was, however, able to complete the Jerry B. Jenkins Christian

Every seed needs to die before it sprouts.

Writers Guild, which was included with my tuition. God used this two-year correspon-dence course to show me that I didn't want to be an overseas missionary, but that He would use my writing to minister to people all over the world. It took many years of healing for me to trust God again with my health, and with moving back to Texas. We moved to Texas with what we could fit in our car, including our dog, Starfish, whom we had adopted six months after we got married.

Shortly after arriving in Austin, we visited the Zilker Botanical Garden and the Dallas Arboretum and Botanic Garden. Unfortunately, we compared both gardens to the NYBG. The Zilker Botanical Garden was too small! The Dallas Arboretum and Botanic Garden was too manicured!

(I should mention that the New York Botanical Garden is rated one of the top gardens in the world. Neither one of them ever stood a chance!)

I had never learned to bloom where I was planted. I was in the mindset that I had to be continually hustling to be happy. (I'll share more of this in Chapter 4.) Personally, I thought this meant moving or going to a new church or traveling to find happiness. Finding beauty under my own two feet was a foreign concept to me. I didn't yet know how to let the grass grow, how to bloom—or even how to dream where I was currently planted. Looking back, I wonder if it's because we didn't have any roots yet as a couple.

Living in Texas afforded us the opportunity to travel and see many gardens. It wasn't until we visited the Houston Arboretum & Nature Center that I had an awakening. While we were walking one of the trails back to our car, I discovered a set of benches. Two of the benches were in the front and the other benches formed a half circle facing them. I was so inspired that I took a picture, which gave me an idea. I thought, "Someday, I will host garden parties." That was my light bulb moment, and God used each garden experience over a process of two years to dream me to life in a garden. See my list below:

1. New York Botanical Garden - Bronx, New York - June, 2014

2. Zilker Botanical Garden - Austin, Texas - April, 2015

3. Dallas Arboretum and Botanic Garden - Dallas, Texas - May, 2015

4. Brooklyn Botanic Garden - Brooklyn, New York - May, 2015

5. Royal Botanic Garden, Kew Gardens - London, England - April, 2016

6. San Diego Botanic Garden - San Diego, California - May, 2016

7. Houston Arboretum & Nature Center - Houston, Texas - May, 2016

8. Denver Botanic Gardens - Denver, Colorado - June, 2016

9. Mercer Botanic Garden - Houston, Texas - October, 2016

10. Bayou Bend Collection and Gardens - Houston, Texas - October, 2016

I needed to cultivate something for the fun of it before realizing God was there waiting to be found. I'm wondering if it's the same for you, too?

With each garden visit, I found a different kind of paradise to linger in unfiltered access to Him. I had no agenda. I was only there to enjoy and take pictures (one of my favorite things). I needed to cultivate something for the fun of it before realizing God was there waiting to be found. I'm wondering if it's the same for you, too? God turned my dream of wanting to see New York into a love for gardens that eventually turned into something personal and deeply spiritual.

"Come tend the soil
Come tend the soil of my soul
And like a garden
And like a garden I will grow
I will grow." (5)

Each dream is a seed waiting to be planted. This is the second spiritual principle of soul gardening.

What makes gardens so special to me is that God took the time to get my attention. In each garden, He was patient and never imposed. I believe it was so that I could discover that *not* every dream planted started with a Bible verse. Like I shared in Chapter 1, if you are cultivating the good soil of the soul, you can rest assured that God is helping you tend your soul garden. He is the One who puts His desires in you before you even plant that first seed in the ground. For me, the seed was a dream waiting to be planted. My dreams were to travel the world and to see New York City. There was nothing spiritual about those two dreams at all. At least *not yet*. They just needed more time. (That'll preach!)

Your Story

Each dream is a seed waiting to be planted. This is the second spiritual principle of soul gardening. Just like a gardener has more than one tool to make his or her garden grow, you now have many tools at your disposal—for a soul that can flourish and grow. I hope you'll be gentle with yourself as you start dreaming up the types of seeds to plant in your soul garden. It takes practice to just...dream. I had to visit

> *Each dream is a seed waiting to be planted. This is the second spiritual principle of soul gardening.*

ten botanical gardens not expecting anything in return. I was just taking time to enjoy life. And that was before the pandemic.

How have you been intentional in the last year or two to get out and enjoy life to find God? Now, more than ever, you and I need wide open spaces to cultivate the soil of our souls.

Ultimately, God is the only one who can give you the courage to tend the soil of your soul and get the conditions ready for dying. It can be a scary process to let go, surrender, and wait on His timing. But I've got news for you. If you're not afraid of your dreams—your dreams are too small! That's why you walk by faith and not by feelings alone.

If you're not afraid of your dreams—your dreams are too small! That's why you walk by faith and not by feelings alone.

I call myself the Dream Defender, but Jesus is the One who's always been in our corner. He is our dream defender. He is the One who helps you and me sow the seeds He's given. It may feel tougher than ever to dream, but that doesn't mean you have to quit or give up before you start. Remember to grow slow. Although every garden (physical and spiritual) starts with one seed, the planting possibilities are endless.

Did you know that God created us to be a variety of vessels? Maybe your physical garden looks more like shabby chic, upcycling, or a simple space on the ground. Spiritually speaking, you might also have bits and pieces you've sown over the years in journals, Bible studies, notes on your computer, or emails you've saved.

Friend, it doesn't matter where you plant but *that* you plant. That's how God sees us, too. You are full of possibility. 2 Timothy 2:20-21 says you can be a special vessel:

"Now in a great house there are not only vessels of gold and silver but also of wood and clay, some for honorable use, some for dishonorable. Therefore, if anyone cleanses himself from what is dishonorable, he will be a vessel for honorable use, set apart as holy, useful to the master of the house, ready for every good work."

I don't know about you, but I want to be useful *and* used for His honor and glory. You are not just a special vessel used by God, but your body holds this same kind of treasure. Your body is a temple where the Holy Trinity resides, including God the Father, Jesus Christ the Son, and His Holy Spirit. Say this out loud with me:

"I am not merely a soul and spirit; I am an embodied human being, and this body is the dwelling place of the Holy Spirit. It is a temple, a place set apart for meeting with God." (6)

> *What a treasure it is to find God in your own broken body. You are not only a special vessel but a temple where you can find God, and He can be found by you.*

What a treasure it is to find God in your own broken body. You are not only a special vessel but a temple where you can find God, and He can be found by you. What a beautiful picture 2 Corinthians 4:7-12 paints:

"But we have this treasure in jars of clay, to show that the surpassing power belongs to God and not to us. We are afflicted in every way, but not crushed; perplexed, but not driven to despair; persecuted, but not forsaken; struck down, but not destroyed; always carrying in the body the death of Jesus, so that the life of Jesus may also be manifested in our bodies.

For we who live are always being given over to death for Jesus's sake, so that the life of Jesus also may be manifested in our mortal flesh. So death is at work in us, but life in you."

I hope those verses above encourage you to read and answer the *Soul Gardening* questions for further reflection below. Remember,

- You are a special vessel.
- You are a temple of the Holy Spirit.
- You are a jar of clay.

I hope you believe this! Before you start writing down every seed that could be a dream that God might want you to plant now or save for later, I hope you won't think too hard. Just start writing in the spaces below. I hope you'll also write down at least five dreams in the journal spaces below or in your own journal to come back to later. In case you're feeling extra vulnerable from the thought of writing down dreams you may never have shared with anyone else, be encouraged from this list from Leeana Tankersley in her book, *Brazen*:

"How dare you dabble.
How dare you romp, frolic, play.
How dare you desire.
How dare you try and fail.
How dare you follow an inkling.
How dare you believe in yourself.
How dare you trust your perceptions.
How dare you see yourself as a reliable observer of this world.

How dare you go big.
How dare you speak up.
How dare you let your gorgeousness off the leash.
How dare you sing.
How dare you paint.
How dare you write.
How dare you make magic.
How dare you love what you offer the world.
How dare you feel fabulous in your own skin.
How dare you take a single step without having it all figured out first.
How dare you let anyone see your holy and holey humanity." (7)

As you wrestle through writing down your dreams today (perhaps for the first time), know you are not alone. Let God stand in the gap for you. Whether He finds you in a busy city like New York, a small town in Iowa (where I now live), or the burbs—let God be your dream defender. Whenever you feel discouraged about your dreams, ask God to open your eyes to see His divine protection. Maybe you're too hooked on human praise (or lack thereof). Maybe you're fighting for your dreams, but God wants to be the One to fight for them—and for you! But first, let me pray for you:

Dear Dream Defender Jesus,

Please don't let me get discouraged when I'm not sure which dreams to write down or which seeds to plant in my soul garden. Help me take my eyes off myself and see the bigger picture. Maybe my dreams can help restore others to health and life. Or maybe what I think is just a small dream that won't help anyone is the beginning of trusting You. I want to know You, Lord. I want to find You in this season—whatever season that may be. Give me hope for the days ahead. Thank You for God-sized confidence in the midst of my weaknesses and doubts. Help me in my unbelief. Help me to see that You are, in fact, enough. Thank You for being my Dream Defender. Sustain me today, I pray, and give me the wisdom to dream with You no matter if I'm in a garden, the privacy of my own home, or my favorite outdoor spot. Amen.

Soul Gardening Questions for Further Reflection

1. What question do you think you need to be asked— whether by God, a mentor, or Life Coach—to help *light a fire* in you and dream you to life again?

_____

_____

_____

_____

_____

_____

_____

_____

_____

_____

2. Did you know there are seven ways to dream with God
    in the garden? There are big, fun, physical, financial,
    emotional, spiritual, and legacy dreams. See the list
    and write down at least five dreams in the spaces
    below.

    a. Big Dreams: Go on a dream vacation; publish a
        book...

    b. Fun Dreams: Ride in a hot air balloon; learn how to
        paint...

    c. Physical Dreams: Lose weight; beat an illness; go
        skydiving...

    d. Financial Dreams: Become debt free; give
        significantly to others...

    e. Emotional Dreams: Overcome fear; forgive a broken
        relationship...

    f. Spiritual Dreams: Go on a ministry conference or
        retreat...

    g. Legacy Dreams: Pass on writings or a ministry you
        started...

    h. Dream#1:_____

    i. Dream#2:_____

    j. Dream#3:_____

    k. Dream#4:_____

    l. Dream#5:_____

3. Did you struggle with writing down at least five dreams? Why or why not? In case you did, here are some of my dreams as examples in case you feel inspired to write a few more dreams down.

    a. Learn to cook from a professional chef

    b. Become a model

    c. Travel to Israel

    d. Learn how to fish

    e. Be a soccer mom

    f. Not get so hungry when I am nervous

    g. Stop running ahead of God, but run with Him

    h. Use my seminary degree to help people find God in every season

    i. Dream#6:_____

    j. Dream#7:_____

4. Have you ever felt afraid to dream with God *or* has God ever used any of your dreams to restore you to health and life? Why? How?

_____

_____

_____

_____

_____

_____

SECTION II

Discover Your Spiritual Season

CHAPTER 3

Each Seed is Planted in the Dark {Winter}

"Anyone who thinks gardening begins in the spring and ends in the fall is missing the best part of the whole year; for gardening begins in January with a dream." (1)

Whenever I visit gardens in the winter, it can be so tempting to say, "There's nothing here to look at. Everything looks dead." Funny enough, the Denver Botanic Garden recently posted a video to educate their social media followers. They were tired of hearing people complain about the "dead" plants in wintertime. The person who created the video took the time to explain that not all plants and trees were "dead," but simply dormant. If I'm honest, I need this reminder, too. *Yes*, some plants do die in the winter, like annuals (plants that last only one season). *Yes*, some perennial plants (plants that live for a few seasons or more) are dormant, but they come back to life.

Maybe you're scratching your head and wondering why I'm starting the spiritual seasons with winter. Let me explain. Most people place the season of spring first. I believe, however, that winter should go before spring. For a seed to come to life or back to life, it needs to be planted in total darkness. Like the beginning of creation when the earth was without form and void (Genesis 1:2). Like the body of Jesus that needed to conquer death before He rose again (Luke 24:46). Just as every winter begins with rest, every fall also ends with rest. Creativity comes after rest, which winter provides along with a slowdown and renewal for the soul.

Are your dreams...waiting for the right time? You might be in a winter spiritual season.

> *Are your dreams... waiting for the right time? You might be in a winter spiritual season.*

To help you dig into the emotions you may be feeling in your winter season, turn to the back of the book and find the "What's in Season?" garden party game. Feel free to mark it up or journal down each word that stands out to you and why you want to cultivate or eradicate it.

Reading the story of Elijah in *Invitation to Solitude and Silence* helped me see that even though my dreams were dormant, they were not dead—they were waiting for the right time. I hope Elijah's story helps you see this, too. Let's read:

> "There he came to a cave and lodged in it. And behold, the word of the Lord came to him, and he said to him, 'What are you doing here, Elijah?' He said, 'I have been very jealous for the Lord, the God of hosts. For the people of Israel have forsaken your covenant, thrown down your altars, and killed your prophets with the sword, and I, even I only, am left, and they seek my life, to take it away.' And he said, 'Go out and stand on the mount before the Lord.' And behold, the Lord passed by, and a great and strong wind tore the mountains and broke in pieces the rocks before

the Lord, but the Lord was not in the wind. And after the wind an earthquake, but the Lord was not in the earthquake. And after the earthquake a fire, but the Lord was not in the fire. And after the fire the sound of a low whisper. And when Elijah heard it, he wrapped his face in his cloak and went out and stood at the entrance of the cave. And behold, there came a voice to him and said, 'What are you doing here, Elijah?'" (1 Kings 19:9-13)

Elijah ran for his life and ended up in a cave. The cave is the place where he asked God to die. I had to sit with the same question that God asked Elijah to discover He was speaking to me through His Word. "What are you doing here, Renee?" He spoke. Take a moment and ask yourself the same question. "What are you doing here, (insert your first name here)?"

God's voice is much softer, slower, and quieter—like a gentle whisper—and requires much patient listening to hear

God's voice is much softer, slower, and quieter—like a gentle whisper—and requires much patient listening to hear Him speak.

Him speak. It was so hard to admit to God that I needed help. Thoughts of suicide, feeling alone, and hopelessness sent me running like Elijah into the cave to find Him. (I'll get to that later in My Story.) The city of Houston, Texas, became a city of refuge where I met the God of Refuge.

God has so many aspects to who He is. To give you an idea of God's most important characteristics to help you through the darkness of a winter spiritual season, I want to share this list by Jen Wilkin in her book, *None Like Him*,

"Theologians make two lists when they describe who God is. One list contains traits that are true only of God. The other contains traits that are true of God but that can also become true of us. Here is an example of such a list: Only God is Infinite, Incomprehensible, Self-Existent, Self-Sufficient, Eternal, Immutable, Omnipresent, Omniscient, Omnipotent, Sovereign. God is (and We Can Be) Holy, Loving, Just, Good, Merciful, Gracious, Long-suffering, Wise, Jealous (for His glory), Faithful, Righteous, True." (2)

How wonderful that He is not only a God who is greater than anything you could ever imagine, but that He is so kind to share some of His attributes with us.

Winter's Miracle

Hearing God's voice was winter's miracle that lit up the darkness in my soul. It allowed me to dream again and to think about what seeds I wanted to sow in the spring. Can you imagine a farmer, after a harvest season, having to go right back to planting? *No way, José!* Those farmers might feel a little bit like Elijah—tired, suicidal from long hours and sleepless nights, or exhausted after keeping up with the harvest. Maybe even all three. Every bit of the farmer's free time in winter is used to fix equipment, plan for the next planting season, and *if* there's time, to rest. Let's be honest. Maybe you choose to rest last because it makes you feel guilty. Or maybe your life is too busy. Plus, after a harvest any crisis, big or small, can send a person running like Elijah. If the farmer needs winter, then, shouldn't we? Zechariah 9:12 says,

"Return to your stronghold, O prisoners of hope;
today I declare that I will restore to you double."

I became a prisoner of hope in winter. One of the ways I did this was using my talent (or gardening tool) of worship. I played and sang worship songs on the keyboard because it took the focus off me and back on God.

I became a prisoner of hope in winter.

Worship helped me win the war and the battle over my mind! I learned how to praise God through the noise and chaos so that I could find Him and hear His voice. Ask yourself, which tragedies are you currently experiencing and which gardening tool can you use to quiet the noise to find God? If you're not currently experiencing a winter spiritual season, ask yourself which tools you used during previous dark days to find Him— or for God to find you.

With Elijah, God wasn't in chaos—He was waiting for Elijah to stand at the mouth of the cave in silence so that He could speak to him. Let me ask you a few more questions:

- ❀ What are you currently afraid of? Is your fear stronger than your faith?

- ❀ Is there anything that is keeping you in tears or currently distracted instead of standing still to hear God's voice?

Every seed is planted in the dark. This is the third spiritual principle of soul gardening. Seeds *have to* be planted in the dark to die in the soil before they will one day grow and turn into a fruitful harvest. One of the most excruciating verses in the Bible says, "'Truly, truly, I say to you, unless a grain of wheat falls into the earth and dies, it remains alone; but if it dies, it bears much fruit'" (John 12:24).

It is okay to not be okay because God will find you—just like He found Elijah in the cave and me in Texas. I needed time to rest in God's presence before I even thought of dreaming again. It was hard, but for me, it was physically sitting in a chair alone with God that helped me overcome my deep, dark nights of the soul. What about you? What would help you, "Sit with your question," and, "Say it out loud" (Ruth Haley Barton)? (3)

My Story

My first spiritual season of winter did not start with a dream. It was quite the opposite. If I had to pick one word to describe winter—it would be *hopeless*. Marc and I found out we were pregnant shortly after moving to Texas. We excitedly told our family and friends only to experience a miscarriage several weeks later. What little hope I had gained from learning to dream in a garden quickly evaporated. I felt alone. Stuck *again*. Despair led us running to Houston months after we closed on our brand-new home in the suburbs of Austin. We quickly sold our home after just four months when Marc accepted a new job in Houston and we relocated to an apartment without a working toilet (we didn't know that until we moved in). Looking back, there were red flags, but God used Marc's job to force us to stay in Houston for one whole year.

I remember going for a walk while I was recovering from my miscarriage. There was this cute couple walking in front of me and the wife was super pregnant. I didn't hear God's

Every seed is planted in the dark. This is the third spiritual principle of soul gardening.

audible voice or anything, but I felt His presence so strongly melting away my fears that I practically dropped to my knees. I didn't want to die. I wanted to live. In my despair, I realized God might be asking me the same question He asked Elijah.

"What are you doing here, Renee?"

As I began to journal the answer to this question, all my anger came spilling out. I believed my sufferings as a child and young adult would carry me through any future dark seasons. *Wrong.* No two seasons are the same. It's the same with spiritual seasons. Some winters are colder and more intense than others. That's what faith is for! I had to go to a very dark place in Houston to tell the truth of what was in my heart. It took me a minute, but I arrived at the conclusion that we were *not* stuck. There was still much to be grateful for. I had to bring my despair to God to hear His voice in my winter season of red flags, the death of an unborn child, and living in a city I hated. In the margin of my Bible next to Elijah's story I wrote:

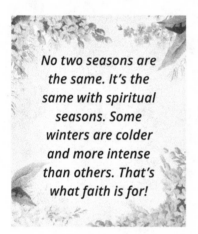

No two seasons are the same. It's the same with spiritual seasons. Some winters are colder and more intense than others. That's what faith is for!

> "I came to Houston to help Marc fulfill his dream calling."

I spent many hours alone with God processing the cockroaches and rats in our second apartment, the dirty sights and smells of Houston from all the rain, Marc's new job that kept him in a state of misery—and the miscarriage. Winter weather might not exist in Houston, but it was during the days of little to no sunlight from all the air pollution that I savored *Invitation to Solitude and Silence* by Ruth Haley Barton. She wrote about Elijah and the cave in a way I had never understood his story before. Houston become like Elijah's cave. I wrote in the margin of my Bible next to Psalm 1,

> "I am in a {Winter} season. The enemy wants to steal my rest by making me believe my dreams are dead, but they are not. I am waiting on spring."

Winter is the season that helped me stop looking busy and important so that I could allow my dreams to awaken. I had to learn that even though I was planting seeds in the dark, my dreams were not dead—they were waiting for the right time. God planted that first seed of what it's actually like to listen and obey with no excuse or blame. Hearing His voice, along with writing down in my Bible that I was in a winter season, allowed me to anticipate what's next: *spring*. I started collecting *all* the things that collectively became the key to get through the spiritual season of winter. Here they are below:

- ❀ *Winter's Pest:* Despair

- ❀ *Winter's Theme:* Hope

- ❀ *Winter's Key Verses:* 1 Kings 19:9, 13 and Zechariah 9:12

- ❀ *Winter's Miracle:* Hearing God's Voice

- ❀ *Winter's Feeling Words:* Abandoned, Alienated, Ashamed, Broken-hearted, Barren, Burdened, Cold, Dark, Depressed, Despair, Disconnected, Doubtful, Dreary, Dry, Empty, Frustrated, Grief, Hopeless,

Hopeful, Humiliated, Insignificant, Isolated, Judged, Lonely, Low, Miserable, Paralyzed, Powerless, Rejected, Restless, Ruined, Stuck, Tired, Trapped, Uncomfortable, Waiting

- *Winter's Prayer:* "Father, I want to honor You and thank You and give You all the glory that You've always given me space to feel what I've been feeling—even when it was scary (as hell). Help me to stop talking, stop doing, and just be in Your Presence. Nothing to do. Nothing to say. Just cultivate rest, peace, and contentment in this winter season. Amen."

- *Winter's Book*: *Invitation to Solitude and Silence* by Ruth Haley Barton

- *Winter's Songs:* "Nothing Shakes the Hope" by First Worship, "Here Now (Madness)" by Hillsong UNITED, "Trust – Live" by Hillsong Young & Free

Your Story

Spiritually speaking, winter is the season when you get to hear—perhaps for the first time—God's still small voice because you're still enough to listen. Winter can sometimes be *the* factor that forces us to stop because it's literally cold outside.

I hope that you'll take the opportunity in this chapter to discover your spiritual season, too. The good news is that it doesn't matter which season you begin with. For me, it was winter. That was the season God found me—and I've been tracking with Him in every season since. I hope that my story in each season helps you discover your spiritual season. I don't know about you, but I want to flourish in every season. To dream where I am planted—no matter what.

In every season, there is a secret key that unlocks the garden of your soul to help you dream again and discover your spiritual season. I am reminded of the book, *The Secret Garden,* by Frances Hodgson Burnett. It was her new friend, the robin, that led Mary Lennox to the locked garden and the key that was hidden nearby, but she had to dig for it. Once Mary let herself in, she realized the garden needed a major cleanup. When she asked for gardening tools from Martha, one of the house servants, they came with the help of a friend, Martha's brother, Dickon. Together, Dickon and Mary brought the beauty of the garden back to life.

If I can be Dickon for a moment, I'd love to show you how to discover your spiritual season. Each of us have a personal journey of the soul to cultivate starting with good soil and planting dream seeds. If you look at nature, each season, physical or spiritual, is different. What worked to help me get through my first dark season to find God as a child was prayer. As a young adult, I learned how to read the Word, which unlocked another dark season. Then, as an adult, it was hearing God's voice for the first time, plus many other avenues, that helped me through my first winter spiritual season. What about you? Here are seven questions to help you "Unlock Your Spiritual Season," which are also listed in the back under Garden Party Games to give you space to write down your answers. I encourage you to ask a friend to answer the same questions so you can share your answers and encourage one another to "be ready in season and out of season" (2 Timothy 4:2).

What seeds have you planted in previous seasons that you are still waiting to see grow? Grab your *Soul Gardening*

What seeds have you planted in previous seasons that you are still waiting to see grow?

tools and let's take advantage of winter's rest. It is my hope that as you take the time to answer the questions above that you'll uncover your secret key to unlock your garden to dream with God and discover your spiritual season.

"Solitude and silence are not self-indulgent exercises for times when an overcrowded soul needs a little time to itself. Rather, they are concrete ways of opening to the presence of God beyond human effort and beyond the human constructs that cannot fully contain the Divine." (4)

Elijah didn't have the strength or the patience to continue. He thought his life was over.

"God has a different read on the whole situation. He says, 'Great! You have now finally left behind all the external trappings that just get in the way on the spiritual journey. You are starting to become empty enough—empty of your reliance on yourself and empty to those things that satisfy only briefly—to begin hungering for a more substantive experience of my presence.'" (5)

Can you imagine the wind, earthquake, and fire weren't enough to satisfy Elijah's deepest hunger? He had just come off a spiritual high. This is usually when winter whips around—immediately following the greatest harvest season ever. Elijah had just called fire down from heaven. It was a God-sized harvest before his very own eyes. In the power of the Holy Spirit, Elijah had just hacked the 450 prophets of Baal to pieces. He was spent physically and spiritually. It is usually when you are spiritually or physically exhausted that you are most vulnerable for physical burnout and a spiritual attack. All it took was *one* death threat by Jezebel to send him running for his life.

Friend, what are you running from? Sometimes the very season that threatens your life becomes *the* door into the divine presence of God, to hear His voice and receive what you need for the journey ahead. Like Elijah, maybe you need to be honest with God. He already knows what's in your heart, even if we don't. I believe this is why God asked Elijah the same question twice!! He couldn't see his own doubt and disbelief. He needed to be gently corrected by God. What about you? If God were to ask you the question, "What are you doing here," how would you answer?

> "We, like Elijah, must walk across the emptiness of the desert 'out there' to arrive at the mouth of the cave that is the emptiness 'in here.' But this is a brave thing to do." (6)

It took me the entire year of living in Houston to learn to tell the truth of what was in my heart. Even if things didn't work out as we originally planned. Even if Marc's job didn't work out. Even if God spared me but took our baby. "Even if." It reminds me of the Bible verse that says, "But *even if* he does not, we want you to know, Your Majesty, that we will not serve your gods or

It is usually when you are spiritually or physically exhausted that you are most vulnerable for physical burnout and a spiritual attack.

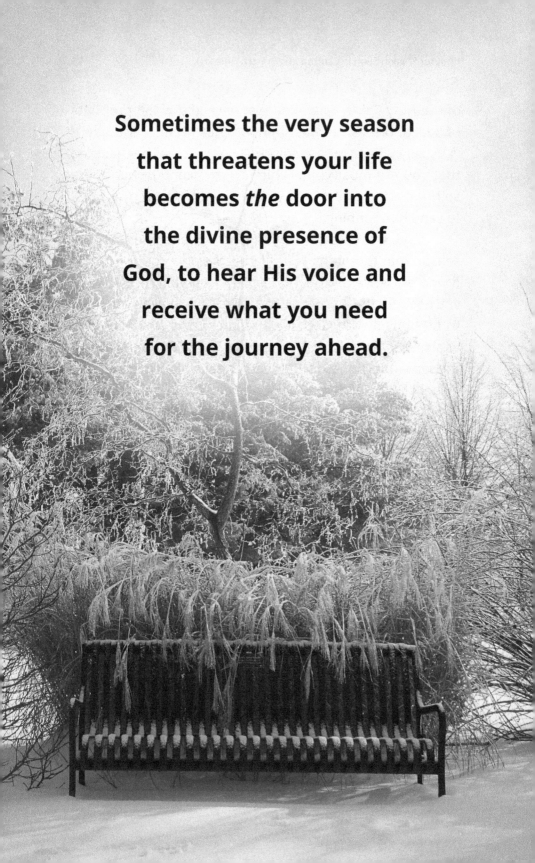

Sometimes the very season
that threatens your life
becomes *the* door into
the divine presence of
God, to hear His voice and
receive what you need
for the journey ahead.

worship the image of gold you have set up" (Daniel 3:18, NIV, *emphasis added*).

Whatever your "even if" might be, I hope you'll speak it out loud. Write it down. Thank you for being brave, even if you don't feel like it. Thank you for admitting the soil of your soul feels empty, and you need rest because you're too weary to dream. He knows you need the break a winter spiritual season can provide because life is messy sometimes. Don't fight the pain. The fact that you're still reading means that you care enough to feel even when it's scary. The good news is, you're still alive, and it's not too late! Speaking of which, if you currently feel in a winter season, the questions may be difficult for you. That is okay. Before you begin answering the many questions I just asked, let me pray for you:

> *The fact that you're still reading means that you care enough to feel even when it's scary. The good news is, you're still alive, and it's not too late!*

Dear Winter Jesus,

Thank You for the story of Elijah in the Old Testament. Thank You that Your Word still speaks today. Help me to see myself in Elijah's story and in his pain and running away. Help me to see that it is never too late to find You—even if it means I'm stuck in a cave of my own making. Set me free today, in Jesus's name. Help me make it through the chaos and confusion to hear Your gentle whisper. Whisper to my heart and expose the lies so that I can speak the truth even if it hurts. Show me the path home. I want to be found by You. I don't want

*to give up. I want to keep living, make it through this
dark season, and dream again. Amen.*

Soul Gardening Questions for Further Reflection

1. What time(s) of the year do you typically search for
    God the most? What triggers it?

_____

_____

_____

_____

_____

_____

_____

2. Where do you enjoy meeting with God the most?
    Indoors? Outdoors? Why?

_____

_____

_____

_____

_____

_____

3. Which characteristic of God that Jen Wilkin mentions
    in her quote are you most drawn to or eager to
    experience? Why?

    _____

    _____

    _____

    _____

    _____

    _____

    _____

    _____

    _____

4. Have you ever heard God's still small voice before?
    If so, what did He say? If not, what is one thing You'd
    most like Him to speak to you about? Pray about it!

    _____

    _____

    _____

    _____

    _____

    _____

    _____

    _____

    _____

5. If you haven't already, take some time now to write your response to the seven questions pertaining to a winter spiritual season below.

   a. What *pest* continues to plague you?

   _____

   _____

   _____

   _____

   _____

   _____

   b. What *theme* is reoccurring in your life right now?

   _____

   _____

   _____

   _____

   _____

   _____

   c. Are there any *Bible verses* that speak life and encouragement into your situation?

   _____

   _____

   _____

   _____

   _____

   _____

d. Have you recently experienced a *miracle*? If so, what was it? How did it make you feel?

_____

_____

_____

_____

_____

_____

_____

e. How are you *feeling* right now?

_____

_____

_____

_____

_____

_____

f. Have you *read* any good books, blogs, or social media posts, or listened to any podcasts?

_____

_____

_____

_____

_____

_____

g. Are there any *songs* that lifted your spirits?

_____

_____

_____

_____

_____

_____

_____

_____

_____

_____

_____

_____

_____

_____

_____

_____

_____

_____

_____

_____

_____

CHAPTER 4

You Cannot Sow and Harvest in the Same Season {Spring}

> "It is divine that God plants a seed in a dark place. Divine. And the whole reason why rain is significant...is because there is a seed. Because, without rain, a seed is not released into the developmental stage." (1)

Imagine with me that you're living in Washington, D.C., and serving the President of the United States. You were selected because you are brave, but you're also disabled. You tell the President that you've found the cure to your debilitating disease, and because he *likes* you—he sends you on Air Force One straight away with cash in hand and a note that says you must be healed. Yeah, that actually happened. In the Bible, I mean. Let's read:

> "Naaman, commander of the army of the king of Syria, was a great man with his master and in high favor, because by him the Lord had given victory to Syria. He was a mighty man of valor, but he was a leper." (2 Kings 5:1)

It's hard to imagine leprosy in today's culture. It was like living a death sentence, only somehow Naaman didn't have to live outside the city and shout, "Unclean, unclean!" every time someone walked by. Yet. His disease must have been in its infancy stage, and he was able to hide it—*for now*. Naaman was also married. His wife had a servant from Israel who told her that if Naaman would only go to her homeland, he could see the prophet and be cured. So, Naaman has a personal chat with the King of Syria and suddenly he's being sent on a quest with money and a letter demanding healing. Let's continue reading:

> "And he brought the letter to the king of Israel, which read, 'When this letter reaches you, know that I have sent to you Naaman my servant, that you may cure him of his leprosy.' And when the king of Israel read the letter, he tore his clothes and said, 'Am I God, to kill and to make alive, that this man sends word to me to cure a man of his leprosy? Only consider, and see how he is seeking a quarrel with me.'" (2 Kings 5:6-7)

That letter was an insult. How does someone demand to be healed of an incurable disease? I've felt the hopelessness of my health issues, and the self-righteousness that demands God heal me because I was being an obedient child. That's called legalism. I wonder if you've felt either one—or both? That even with the best doctors and prayer-warring friends and family, the Lord doesn't guarantee healing. In fact, your quest has gotten you into a bit of a pickle. Not only have you insulted those trying to help you, but you've audaciously required that you...will...be... healed.

When Elisha the prophet heard that the king of Israel had torn his clothes, he sent word to the king to send

Naaman to him so "that he may know that there is a prophet in Israel" (2 Kings 5:8b). This was where the story caught my attention—like King James style, "Thus saith the Lord," kind of attention.

When Naaman arrived, Elisha sent his servant to tell Naaman to dip in the Jordan River seven times. He didn't even come to the door to say hello. Elisha knew Naaman's pride. Maybe it was because he had the presumption to think he could demand healing. Maybe it was because he thought his position and power made him more important than others, which demanded a response. Or worse, maybe he didn't respect the Lord's omnipotence. Regardless, Elisha knew the circumstances, because God had revealed the source of this man's illness, and he knew that only God could make a man [or woman] "alive."

Naaman was furious. He went into a rage and whined like a little baby, threatening to get back on Air Force One, I mean, jump back on his horse and bolt home. When Elisha did not come to the door, but sent his servant instead—Naaman was insulted. How dare Elisha not cater to him? After all, he was a VIP (very important person), and he knew it (which makes it worse). To add insult to injury, Elisha's servant gave him a disgusting command to bathe in an "unclean" river. Naaman was basically standing with his nose up against a shut door with servants behind him quaking in their boots because of Naaman's temper.

But, his servants had the courage to say something that changed the course of his life—and mine—forever. Listen:

> "And his servants came near, and spake unto him, and said, My father, if the prophet had bid thee do some *great thing*, wouldest thou not have done it? how

much rather then, when he saith to thee, Wash, and be clean?" (2 Kings 5:13, KJV, *emphasis added*)

Only in the King James Version does it mention the words "great thing." Did you catch that? That's what made this verse so powerful to me. God didn't need Naaman to do a "great thing" to receive His healing. God doesn't need me to do a "great thing" to receive His healing in my life either—and neither do you. In her book, *Breaking the Fear Cycle*, Maria Furlough writes, "Do you focus in so closely on wishing God would bless you at work with job security, a raise, or a new position, while he is working on a greater thing to be done in the lives of the people working around you?" (2)

> *God doesn't need you to do "great things" for Him and His kingdom. It's actually the other way around.*

God doesn't need you to do "great things" for Him and His kingdom. It's actually the other way around. Let's rewind and imagine a different ending—kind of like when a good movie gives you a different or surprise ending. Let's say Elisha comes to the door and coddles Naaman's ego. He bows down and practically worships the guy because he's in "high favor," which comes with a load of money, a title, and all that. Elisha waves some magic words and says, "Thus says the Lord," and suddenly, before everyone's eyes, Naaman is healed. His leprosy disappears. Just like that. Elisha pockets the money and even gains notoriety and fame.

Nope. That is not how God works.

As a recovering people-pleaser, I can relate to the truth of this story. Proverbs 29:25 says, "The fear of man lays a snare, but whoever trusts in the LORD is safe." Matthew 19:26 says, "'With man this is impossible, but with God all things are possible.'" What *does* happen is that Naaman flies into a rage because his secret hopes for healing in a dramatic fashion have been dashed—or so he thinks. They didn't come to fruition instantly like he had imagined.

What will Naaman do next? Let's re-read verse 13.

> "My father, if the prophet had bid thee do some *great thing*, wouldest thou not have done it? how much rather then, when he saith to thee, Wash, and be clean." (2 Kings 5:13, KJV, *emphasis added*)

Somehow these words help Naaman count to ten and calm down. He regroups, humbles himself, and decides to go down to the Jordan River, which is considered to be "unclean," and have a bath. Seven of them. I find it interesting that God sends Naaman, the "unclean" leper, to the most "unclean" river for healing.

Often, the one thing that can cure and heal you is the one thing you fear most. Job knew a thing or two about that when he wrote, "For the thing that I fear comes upon me, and what I dread befalls me" (Job 3:25).

> *Often, the one thing that can cure and heal you is the one thing you fear most.*

Thank God that's not the end of the story for Naaman, Job, me, or you. God has the final word! Naaman obeys, takes seven baths in the Jordan, and immediately comes out clean like a baby. End of story.

Now that's a pretty picture, isn't it? Healing! Clean! Fresh! New! *This* is God's doing. *This* is how He works.

> *You can tell whether your healing is from God if it brings freedom and healing. If it doesn't—chances are it's not from Him.*

You can tell whether your healing is from God if it brings freedom and healing. If it doesn't—chances are it's not from Him. Don't let anyone tell you otherwise. It took me a while to learn how to pull back from my own expectations and demands—like Naaman—but with it came the freedom to discover how to go deeper with God while waiting on Him for all I needed to live a daily life—not just the dream of healing.

Spring's Miracle

Let's pause there for now and pick the story back up later. Are your dreams...*preparing to sprout?* You might be in a spring spiritual season. If you're unsure of which emotions you may or may not be feeling, turn to the back of the book and find the "What's in Season?" garden party game. Feel free to mark it up or journal down each word that stands out to you and why you want to cultivate or eradicate it.

> *Are your dreams.. preparing to sprout? You might be in a spring spiritual season.*

You cannot sow and harvest in the same season. This is the fourth spiritual principle of soul gardening.Oftentimes when God speaks a word, you don't see its manifestation right away. A seed needs darkness, rain, fertile ground, and heat to sprout. God provides all of these "great things." This is not something you can

You cannot sow and harvest in the same season. This is the fourth spiritual principle of soul gardening.

do on your own. He brings the growth (see 1 Corinthians 3:6-7). He expects you to wait and be patient like the farmer (see James 5:17-18). This is why you cannot place your demands or expectations on God for the seeds you are hoping for, including seeds He's promised to sprout. But, why is that?

Let's look once again at the life of Elijah, who we read about in the last chapter. Only this time, we're going to learn a lesson from him *before* he ran for his life into a cave.

> "After many days the word of the Lord came to Elijah, in the third year, saying, 'Go, show yourself to Ahab, and I will send rain upon the earth.' So Elijah went to show himself to Ahab. Now the famine was severe in Samaria.'" (1 Kings 18:1-2)

While you are waiting for your seeds to sprout and grow, here are three ways to monitor your soul growth. Ask yourself which stage you're currently in:

1. *Visitation* - You hear things you cannot see yet.

2. *Supplication* - You spend time in deep and focused prayer.

3. *Expectation* - You see an outward showing of the seed and don›t stop looking forward to the fruition of the promise of God. (3)

"Any time God speaks a word in your life—how many of you know the exact opposite is actually happening when you receive that word? And the reason why that happens is actually agricultural as well as spiritual." (4) I don't know about you, but I don't like getting caught in the rain. I don't like getting my hair or clothes wet. Spiritually speaking, I also struggle when God pours rain on my seeds. I often feel like I'm drowning because I'm too focused on the rain puddles instead of all the blessings of the rain.

In Bible times, the rain was significant because it meant God's blessing. The same is true today. You and I need rain in order to grow. All seeds grow through dark, messy, and wet soil. Israel was an agricultural society. They needed rain in order for their crops to thrive and provide food for their nation. The same is true spiritually. In order for the seeds that have been dormant in winter to come to life in the spring, you need to go through a "rainy" period that cleanses and heals you. I encourage you not to give up while you are waiting for the manifestation of the promises of God. Let me share my story with you in the hopes of encouraging you to keep waiting on the miracle you're desperately praying for.

In Bible times, the rain was significant because it meant God's blessing. The same is true today. You and I need rain in order to grow.

My Story

"My healing will not come from a 'great thing,'" I wrote in the margin of my Bible on January 22, 2018, next to 2 Kings 5:13 and the story of Naaman. Marc and I had just finished our year in Houston and had moved back to Austin. We no longer felt stuck. He had gotten a new job, and I was writing a new book on fear. God had also helped me grieve my miscarriage, find release from the grief, and plant new seeds in the hope that we would be parents. Things were looking up. In fact, I was feeling so good that I went off my anxiety medication. It wasn't an easy decision. I prayed and sought the Lord and wise counsel and didn't let fear stand in my way as it had before.

God had changed me in a new way. Surely, this was God's way of healing me to get pregnant again. I weaned off the medication slowly with the help of my doctor, but instead of being healed, I began to experience terrible withdrawal symptoms and my panic attacks returned. They were so bad that I had to go back on my medication and vowed that was the *last* time I would attempt to do that again. I now know how Paul felt when he begged God to remove his thorn three times. In the last decade, I've attempted to go off my anxiety medication three times—and each time God said, "No."

The story of Naaman touched my soul. I had been trying to gain God's favor without realizing I had set certain demands for my healing that made me miss the one thing that God said to do. Or actually *not* to do. After much prayer, I realized that God never said He was going to heal me of my anxiety, but He did promise me in His Word that, "yes," we would be parents on this side of heaven. That realization hit me like a ton of bricks. I knew then that God was going to bless us with children—it just wasn't going to come as a result of something *I did*, but something *He would do* for me.

> *I believe God's promises are not a result of something you'll do but something He will do for you.*

I believe God's promises are not a result of something you'll do but something He will do for you. Like the rain He provides for the seeds to sprout. It was Naaman's story that helped me to discover the physical and spiritual meaning of Psalm 126:5 that says:

"Those who sow in tears
shall reap with shouts of joy!"

My healing would not come in the same season I planted in tears. For the first time in my life, I understood that I could not sow and harvest in the same season. I needed the messy, wet spiritual season of spring where everything was sprouting, but I wasn't sure yet what would turn into summer fruit.

"When we try to bypass the vehicle of the Holy Spirit and release our gifts to the world, we end up dwelling on our own insecurities. When we are obedient to give our gifts over to the Lord and the power of the Holy Spirit, He releases them to the world." (5)

Unlike the story of Elijah that we read about in Chapter 3, this time God was in the rain. Yes, He allowed wind, earthquakes, and fire to get Elijah's attention in 1 Kings 19, but God was not in any of those things except for the sound of a "low whisper." This time, in 1 Kings 18, we read that not only was God *in* the fire, but also the rain. God enables Elijah to call fire down from heaven, kill the prophets of Baal, and pray for rain to return after a three-year famine until he sees a cloud the size of a man's hand. Let's read:

"Now Elijah said to Ahab, 'Go up, eat and drink; for there is the sound of the roar of a *heavy* shower.' So Ahab went up to eat and drink. But Elijah went up to the top of Carmel; and he bent down to the earth and put his face between his knees. And he said to his servant, 'Go up now, look toward the sea.' So he went up and looked, but he said, 'There is nothing.' Yet *Elijah* said, 'Go back' seven times. And *when he returned* the seventh *time*, he said, 'Behold, a cloud as small as a person's hand is coming up from the sea.'" (1 Kings 18:41-44a, NASB)

If God speaks a word—it will *happen.*

If God speaks a word—it *will* happen. Elijah knew this, and he was willing to pray seven times, just as Naaman (eventually) dipped in the Jordan River seven times to see the completion of God's word to him. In my spring season, I needed the cloud from 1 Kings 18 that turned into much-needed rain as a reminder to pray without ceasing, plant in tears, and not give up. Below I listed all the things that helped me unlock and experience spring's miracle of healing, knowing it would not happen the way I demanded or expected—or even in the same season.

- ❀ *Spring's Pest:* Fear

- ❀ *Spring's Theme:* Peace

- ❀ *Spring's Key Verses:* 2 Kings 5:13, 1 Kings 18, Psalm 126:5

- ❀ *Spring's Miracle:* Healing

- ❀ *Spring's Feeling Words:* Alive, Amazed, Aware, Beautiful, Blooming, Cautious, Confused, Chaotic, Creativity, Excitement, Expectancy, Delight, Fearful, Forgiveness, Growth, Healthy, Humility, Impatience, Messy, Noisy, Nurturing, Purpose, Tempted, Painful, Peaceful, Refined, Spontaneous, Sprouting, Trusting, Vulnerable, Warming Up

⊛ *Spring's Prayer:* "Dear Father, I don't have to prove anything to You by keeping a ritual that makes me irritable. I don't have to earn Your approval. I am Your Daughter. I am adopted into Your family. The feeling I have experienced recently is peace. Lord, help me cultivate rest in this spring season. Amen."

⊛ *Spring's Book*: *Awaken* by Priscilla Shirer

⊛ *Spring's Songs:* "There is a Cloud" by Elevation Worship, "Glimpse" by Kim Walker-Smith, "Do it Again" by Elevation Worship, "Be Still" by The Fray, "Lay it All Down" by Will Reagan & United Pursuit, "Not in a Hurry" by Will Reagan & United Pursuit

What about you? What cloud are you currently praying for and waiting to appear? I was too weak to plant a seed in the ground for another child in my winter season. I needed winter's rest to awaken my dream of one day having a baby. In my spring season, I deposited that seed in the dark and thought it would happen in that *same* season—only to learn that my tears were the rain it needed to develop. I had to let go of the seed I had planted and leave the results to God to make it sprout.

Farmers know that after they've planted their seeds, their job is done. Finished. Exodus 14:14 says, "The LORD shall fight for you, and ye shall *hold your peace*" (KJV, *emphasis added*). Farmers know how to "hold their peace" and wait for the spring rains and summer heat before collecting the harvest. This is a physical as well as spiritual principle.

I don't know which parts of this chapter resonate with you, but the hardest part for me was in letting go. I had no idea how many weeks, months, or years it would be—before

God would heal my body to conceive another baby. I had to be willing to plant the seed in the dark, watch it die, water it with my tears, and continue living life as a barren wife, which—if I'm honest—feels like the modern-day equivalent of being a leper.

Your Story

"Every seed, buried in sorrow
You will call, forth in its time
You are Lord, Lord of the harvest
Calling our hope, now to arise
We receive Your rain
We receive Your rain
We receive Your rain
We receive Your rain." (6)

Reading the story of Naaman and learning about the spiritual significance of rain helped me see that even though my dreams were sprouting, they were not ready for harvest yet—they were waiting for a later season.

Friend, do you know if you are in a spring spiritual season? Have you planted in tears after resting during the winter? I just love what Priscilla Shirer writes in her book, *Awaken,* about this same cloud that Elijah prayed for:

"In 1 Kings 18, during the reign of wicked King Ahab and the oppression of a three-year drought, most Israelites scanning the western sky would think the tiny wisp of a cloud 'as small as a man's hand' (v. 44) was nothing to get too excited about. It didn't even qualify as an official cloud really. More of a cloud fragment, a cloud baby, hoping it could grow up to actually be a cloud someday. Yet to ears like the prophet Elijah's, which were tuned in to heaven's frequency, this hazy puff of moisture in the heavens had 'the sound of the roar of a heavy shower' (v. 41). To eyes looking for more than the average answers to average prayers, it wouldn't be long before 'the sky grew black with clouds and wind' (v. 45) and God's awesome rain-making ability would be put on full, drenching display." (7)

Learning about the rain inspired me to keep praying until my own cloud baby appeared. Naaman's story of healing encouraged me to wait on God for my spring miracle to manifest—even though that meant I wouldn't see it until later. I hope you'll take some time to pray, journal, and reflect on what might be your spring miracle. Before you begin answering the many questions below to discover the key to unlock your spring spiritual season, let me pray for you:

Dear Spring Jesus,

Thank You for the story of Naaman in the Old Testament. I know that whatever miracle I am waiting and praying for—if You have promised it to me—will happen even if I have to wait until the fall. Help me to persevere in prayer, like Elijah, knowing that the cloud will appear at some point. Even if it doesn't, I pray You will enlighten my soul and tune it to Your desires so that when I pray—You answer. Simple as that. I don't want to pray for something You haven't promised. I want to see this cloud come to manifestation in my life, and it has to come from You, because what is impossible with man is possible only with You. You are the rainmaker, my Healer, and Friend. I love You. Thank You for hearing and answering my prayers. Amen.

Soul Gardening **Questions for Further Reflection**

1. What does rain mean to you? Are you a "dance in the
    rain" kind of person or would you rather stay indoors,
    curl up, and read or just rest? No matter how you feel
    about the rain, take some time to ask God to show
    you a fresh revelation of His spiritual rain in your life
    and how He might want to use that rain to grow and
    develop your soul.

    _____

    _____

    _____

    _____

    _____

    _____

    _____

2. Have you ever tried to do a "great thing" for God? What
    was the outcome? Has God ever done a "great thing"
    in your life? Have you ever felt filled with His joy or
    planted in tears? Read Psalm 126:1-6 and journal your
    responses below.

    _____

    _____

    _____

    _____

_____

_____

_____

3. Have you ever tried to plant and harvest in the same season, physically or spiritually? What were the results? What did you learn?

_____

_____

_____

_____

_____

_____

4. Is there currently a cloud in your life that you are praying and waiting to see the manifestation of?

_____

_____

_____

_____

_____

_____

5. Take some time to write your response to the seven questions pertaining to a spring spiritual season below.

   a. What *pest* continues to plague you?

_____

_____

b. What *theme* is reoccurring in your life right now?

_____

_____

_____

c. Are there any *Bible verses* that speak life and encouragement into your situation?

_____

_____

_____

_____

_____

_____

_____

_____

_____

_____

_____

d. Have you recently experienced a *miracle*? If so, what was it? How did it make you feel?

_____

_____

_____

_____

_____

_____

_____

_____

_____

_____

_____

_____

e. How are you *feeling* right now?

_____

_____

f. Have you *read* any good books, blogs, or social media posts, or listened to any podcasts?

_____

_____

_____

_____

_____

_____

g. Are there any *songs* that lifted your spirits?

_____

_____

_____

_____

_____

_____

CHAPTER 5

Ripe Fruit Bruises Easily {Summer}

"God ordained the seasons and God ordained time (cf. Genesis 1:14), and as the seasons do indeed continue to cycle through, one after another, we can take some comfort in the continual evidence of God's sovereignty expressed in the unchangeable mutability of the weather." (1)

How's the weather where you live? I hope you find it ironic that I waited until Chapter 5 to ask you a question about the weather. (I'm not really a small talk kind of girl). If there's one thing I know—seasons are divine, and they each have their "appointed time." Their progress and cycles go in order because that is the way God created them (Genesis 1:14).

Sometimes, you pray for God to move you to a better, more flourishing season but don't recognize His provision when the time arrives in your current season. Maybe that's why you often say to others, "This too shall pass." That statement is partially true but doesn't always offer comfort to someone who is struggling

Seasons are divine, and they each have their "appointed time."

with blooming (or not blooming) where they are planted. Being mindful of the weather, you can learn a few more substantial things to say to others—including yourself—to be encouraged by:

- ❀ *You can stand on God's Word.* If you are struggling, remember, it's just a season. It *will* pass. "The grass withers, the flower fades, but the word of our God will stand forever" (Isaiah 40:8).

- ❀ *You can have peace in God.* If the rhythm of your spiritual life feels out of whack, God can create physical order out of spiritual messes. "For God is not a God of disorder, but of peace" (1 Corinthians 14:33, NLT).

- ❀ *You can keep asking God.* It's okay to ask for help. What works in one season may not work in another. Ask God, who "changes times and seasons" (Daniel 2:21a).

- ❀ *You can look to God.* If it doesn't take much effort to understand the weather and act accordingly, how much more can you learn spiritual things by looking to God (Matthew 16:2-3; Luke 12:54-56)?

Each one of the four spiritual seasons in *Soul Gardening* is meant to teach you how to understand the God who created seasons and what He wants to teach you before the next one comes. It doesn't matter what spiritual season of life you currently find yourself in because I have good news for you:

You cannot miss your "appointed time."

Are your dreams...*ready for harvest?* You might be in a summer spiritual season. If you're unsure of which emotions you may or may not be feeling, turn to the back of the book and find the "What's in Season?" garden party game.

Are your dreams...
ready for harvest?
You might be in
a summer
spiritual season.

Feel free to mark it up or journal down each word that stands out to you and why you want to cultivate or eradicate it.

You were created with a purpose to bear fruit for eternity. This is how you know that you are ready for summer, *because* you faithfully plowed through to the good soil of your soul *and* planted seeds in obedience, not knowing which ones might sprout. But what happens if you were too afraid to plant any seeds in the spring? Let's read:

> "Does a farmer always plow and never sow? Is he forever cultivating the soil and never planting?" (Isaiah 28:24, NLT)

I sure hope not! If the farmer only plowed his land and never planted any seed in the spring, he'd miss out on the harvest in a later season. The farmer doesn't have time to worry about the heat or the pests that seem to multiply in the summer. The farmer knows that if seed is not planted in the ground in the spring—absolutely *nothing* will grow. What about you? Do you still need help to plant the seeds you were too afraid to plant in your spring spiritual season? It's okay. I understand (see Summer's Miracle below).

Summer's Miracle

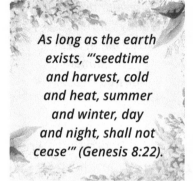

As long as the earth exists, "'seedtime and harvest, cold and heat, summer and winter, day and night, shall not cease'" (Genesis 8:22).

I have a confession to make. I buried a seed in my spring spiritual season of the "appointed time" instead of planting it, because I was too afraid to let it die. Thank God my fear and disobedience didn't stop summer's miracle. God blessed that seed, even though I waited to plant it in the summer. I can't believe God blessed my delayed obedience because that one Hebrew word changed my life, and I hope it changes yours too. Let's read:

> ✦ "For everything there is a season, and a *time* for every matter under heaven." (Ecclesiastes 3:1, *emphasis added*)

> ✦ "You will arise and have pity on Zion; it is the time to favor her; the *appointed time* has come." (Psalm 102:13, *emphasis added*)

The Hebrew word "season" in Ecclesiastes 3:1 means "time." (2) The Hebrew word for "appointed time" in Psalm 102:13 means "seasons." (3) I discovered, by surprise, that those two Hebrew words are *not* the same. The key lies in Genesis 1:14:

> "And God said, 'Let there be lights in the expanse of the heavens to separate the day from the night. And let them be for signs and for *seasons*, and for days and years'" (*emphasis added*).

This is prophetic! The significance of "seasons" in the Bible meaning "appointed time" opened my eyes to see that I cannot miss what God has promised—even if the harvest does not come when I hope or expect! As long as the earth exists, "'seedtime and harvest, cold and heat, summer and winter, day and night, shall not cease'" (Genesis 8:22).

Many of Jesus's parables, including famous Bible stories, connect the weather to soul growth.

Let me ask you a question. Have you ever experienced time in both ways? Many of Jesus's parables, including famous Bible stories, connect the weather to soul growth. Jesus is quoted twice in the Gospels talking about the seasons:

⚘ "He replied, 'When evening comes, you say, "It will be fair weather, for the sky is red," and in the morning, "Today it will be stormy, for the sky is red and overcast." You know how to interpret the appearance of the sky, but you cannot interpret the signs of the times.'" (Matthew 16:2-3, NIV)

⚘ "He said to the crowd: 'When you see a cloud rising in the west, immediately you say, "It's going to rain," and it does. And when the south wind blows, you say, "It's going to be hot," and it is. Hypocrites! You know how to interpret the appearance of the earth and the sky. How is it that you don't know how to interpret this present time?'" (Luke 12:54-56, NIV)

It doesn't take much effort to walk outside and determine if it's going to rain that day. It does, however, take time

God imprinted a divine order
of the four seasons in nature
so you can trust in Him and His
"appointed time" in your life.

to flourish and accept the fact that you might be focused on *one* version of time when God is more concerned with the other—His "appointed time." God imprinted a divine order of the four seasons in nature so you can trust in Him and His "appointed time" in your life.

My Story

I experienced time in both of the two ways mentioned above when I was eleven years old. Every memory I have proceeding up to the morning my anxiety started in March of 1993 is clouded—foggy at best. It was the first *time* my parents had traveled together without us kids for longer than a few days. I watched as their shuttle van left our driveway and then walked back to the house with my brother and our adopted grandma, who was taking care of us while they were away on a mission trip. Something inside of me broke. A dam of tears hit me like a tidal wave of anxiety that never left. Suddenly, I was afraid to be without my parents. I couldn't stop crying. My body began experiencing anxiety that I had never felt before. All of this happened in a matter of seconds as we walked outside to say goodbye to my parents. Through my watery eyes, I spied a shadowy figure of a cat.

A cat!

I had asked my dad numerous times for a cat, and each time he said no. That was my first-ever prayer request I remember asking God for as a child. That morning, I looked up on the roof and called the cat down. I can't believe he stayed with us the whole time my parents were away. My brother and I named him Lemon, but he was really mine.

That day, I experienced *time* in two different ways, as "time" being just another day and also as God's "appointed time." Not only did God answer my prayer for a cat, but He waited until *the* day my battles with anxiety began. This brought me much comfort. What is even more significant is that Lemon stayed with me for the next seven years through the worst of my health issues.

I share this story because I know I'm not the only one who is afraid to ask God for what you really want, which in my case was a cat. The waiting felt like forever, but when God answered in His perfect timing, the waiting made sense, including when God chose to answer that prayer. I also know I'm not the only one who has experienced God's "appointed time" during the midst of a crisis, which in my case was a mental health crisis.

It's often hard to decipher when God is speaking some-thing prophetic or significant when the heat of summer is beating down on you. Maybe your summer pest is fear, anger, or apathy. Whatever it is, I hope you won't be afraid tell others *in* the season He spoke to you even if you don't have everything figured out yet.

I did a recent poll on my social media and asked the question, "Do others know your dreams?" Seventy-five percent of the people who voted said no. At first, I was shocked, but if I'm hon-est—I can relate. I felt like my dreams of being a profes-sional author had failed. My first book, *Faithbook of Jesus* (published under my maiden name), sold out the first print run before its release date. Because of the success of my

> When I was afraid, God renewed my soul and set me back on the path to discovering my spiritual season. I believe He wants to do this for you, too.

first book, I was immediately offered a two-book contract by another publishing house for *Not Another Dating Book* and *Forgiving Others, Forgiving Me.* Unfortunately, they both sold poorly and were quickly discontinued. My publishing career was over—or so I thought. My dreams of writing were shattered until God opened the doors to self-publishing. I felt like such a fraud because I was still afraid to share what God was really putting on my heart years later when He gave me the prophetic word on "appointed time." It wasn't until I read *Whispers and Wildflowers* by Sarah Beth Marr that I understood the meaning of Mark 4:20, which helped me release the "appointed time" seed I had been holding on to for over a year. It says:

> "But those that were sown on the good soil are the ones who hear the word and accept it and bear fruit, thirtyfold and sixtyfold and a hundredfold."

I wrote in the margin of my Bible next to this verse, "I am still in a spring season, but I am waiting for summer!" I also wrote down four points to help me remember what to do next time I wanted to hold on to my seed:

1. Hear the word
2. Accept it
3. Release it
4. Bear fruit

I knew, after reading Mark 4:20, that I needed to release control of my literary career and give it over to God so that I could once again bear fruit. I was not, nor will I ever be, in charge of the harvest. Sarah Beth Marr writes:

"One thing I've learned about the Word through the years of my own growing is that it settles, satisfies, and renews my soul. It's the perfect soul-nourishment. The Word makes my soul right again." (4)

When I was afraid, God renewed my soul and set me back on the path to discovering my spiritual season. I believe He wants to do this for you, too. I knew what I needed to do with the prophetic word on the seasons. I needed to accept what God gave me and release it so that He would bear fruit through me—even if it wasn't in the same season God gave it to me. I confessed my sins to God, and asked Him for a second chance to plant the seed. I'm so glad He forgave me and blessed that seed.

Can I be honest for a moment? I knew when those two books didn't sell well that my publisher wouldn't offer me another book contract. If they *had* offered me another book contract, I wouldn't have been able to say no—even though God hadn't placed another idea for a book on my heart. The truth is, I was more bruised by the sting of rejection (not getting another contract) than the fact that God hadn't yet spoken a fresh word for another book.

Ouch.

Let me say that again. I would have done anything, said anything, and made up something to stay a traditionally-published author. That's the danger of counterfeit summer fruit. It wouldn't have tasted sweet or ripe. I would have said yes for all for the wrong reasons, simply to continue writing and posting in the spotlight. God had to humble me and show me that my books *did* reach people. And even if my books didn't reach as many people as my publisher would have hoped, those people were the people God intended for me to reach. It wasn't about selling more books, but about being faithful and true to the words He had already given me while waiting for another fruitful summer season. I know that now.

It wasn't until I read that one small Hebrew word on the "appointed time" that I knew this was it. God had spoken a fresh word. In my summer spiritual season, I was able to hear, accept, and release the word on "seasons." Most authors and creatives have to live the word that God gives

> *You can't miss your "appointed time" because God created the "seasons," and He's in charge. The harvest belongs to Him.*

them first before releasing it to the world. I believe this with my whole heart because I've lived, failed, and tried again. You can't miss your "appointed time" because God created the "seasons," and He's in charge. The harvest belongs to Him.

I didn't know this one seed from one Hebrew word would turn into the book you're now reading in your hands, but I knew I was being obedient to release it to the world when God told me to. I'm grateful that I didn't hide it, because over the years my scraps have deepened to include further revelations that I shared on social media and blog posts, all while enjoying each new garden I visited. When I started hosting online garden parties, I had a feeling God was just getting started!

In my summer season, I needed to unlock all of the things below to experience summer's miracle of continued healing—and not just in becoming a mother in the future, but trusting God with the bruises from my writing career as well—knowing He is the One who called me to write and spur others forward (Hebrews 10:24).

✤ *Summer's Pest:* Release Control

✤ *Summer's Theme:* Fruitfulness

✤ *Summer's Key Verses:* Mark 4:20; Psalm 102:13; Genesis 1:14; Galatians 5:22-23

✤ *Summer's Miracle:* Planting the "Appointed Time" Seed

✤ *Summer's Feeling Words:* Restlessness, Guilt, Shame, Softening, Satisfied, Savoring, Relaxing, Enjoying, Sunshine, Renewal, Maturing, Forthright, Ripe, Repentance, Holy, Righteousness, Character, Faithful, Forward, Clean, Healing, Pleasure, Goodness, Remember, Playful, Movement, Enlarge, Hot

✤ *Summer's Prayer:* "Dear Father, I thank You for refreshing me in this summer season and for reminding me to count my blessings even before the harvest to help me cultivate contentment. I am thankful for Your ultimate sacrifice, which allows me to seek Your face daily—whenever I want. I draw near with a full heart of gratitude and love for what You have already done for me. Help me to remember You in this season of rest and peace. Amen."

✤ *Summer's Book*: *Whispers and Wildflowers* by Sarah Beth Marr

✤ *Summer's Songs:* "Glorious" (feat. Skylar Grey) by Macklemore, "Love Won't Let Me Down" by Hillsong Young & Free, "Till the End of Time" by Code Carnes and Kari Jobi

I'm glad I released what God was doing and the prophetic word on "seasons"—even if I didn't have it all figured out yet. What about you? Are you still stuck in the last spiritual season? Is there a seed that you're still holding on to or have hidden somewhere? God wants you, as He did with me, to release it. Confess your sins

Confess your sins and let the seed go, friend.

and let the seed go, friend. You and I need only to be available. To be ready for harvest. He is the One to bear fruit in and through us, as we'll see in the next chapter.

In my summer season, I gave God my brokenness only to be welcomed into His loving arms. Once again, I had to let go of the seed that I thought I had planted, plant it for real this time—and leave the results to God. My soul was growing.

Your Story

It can be hard to let go of the seeds you want to plant because of previous unmet longings or differed hopes and dreams. Ripe fruit bruises easily. This is the fifth spiritual principle of soul gardening. Summer can so easily burn and bruise—not just because of the hot sun, but because fruit actually softens as it ripens. (And don't forget about all the pests that devour what's already ripe.) All of the sugars in the summertime increase exponentially to help the fruit soften, which attracts animals and people alike to partake and eat.

Have you ever purchased a perfect peach or (insert your favorite summer fruit here) and accidentally dropped it? I have. By the time I pick it up, cut out the bruise, and take a bite—I have peach juice streaming down my chin because the bruised fruit is so ripe and soft. But because the fruit tastes good, I don't waste what's left even if it means I have to cut out the bruise.

Dear friend, this is a picture of your heart. The closer you get to Jesus and the harvest He has planned for you, the easier it is to take offense, get hurt, and want to close yourself off and hide before you're fully ripe. Maybe your version of hiding is thinking that if you share the message God has put on your heart, someone will steal it, copy it, or become jealous of it. You're not ready to handle the pressure! Or maybe your version of hiding is to spray every pest who comes near you with Roundup.

> "For we do not wrestle against flesh and blood, but against the rulers, against the authorities, against the cosmic powers over this present darkness, against the spiritual forces of evil in the heavenly places." (Ephesians 6:12)

It's easy to focus on your bruises, I know, but what if the battle you are fighting isn't against the pests of this world? Maybe you are closer to the harvest than you think. Maybe that broken heart, bruised ego, or shattered places are there because God has done a miracle in you already—you just can't see it yet. Just like the expression, "Don't throw the baby out with the bathwater," I say, "Don't throw your life away because of your bruises."

You are ripening, friend! You just may not know it yet.

You *are* ripening, friend! You just may not know it yet. This is why you have to take up the whole armor of God (see Ephesians 6:10-18).

Ripe fruit bruises easily.
This is the fifth spiritual
principle of soul gardening.

Oftentimes, the kind of fruit that God is preparing to bear through you looks different from the world's fruit. Paul writes in Galatians 5:22-23:

"But the fruit of the Spirit is love, joy, peace, patience, kindness, goodness, faithfulness, gentleness, self-control; against such things there is no law."

> *Don't be surprised if your bruises begin multiplying as the fruit of Spirit exponentially increases in your life making you more like Him.*

Don't be surprised if your bruises begin multiplying as the fruit of Spirit exponentially increases in your life making you more like Him. God knows the perfect time to harvest everything He's been doing in your life up to this point. He is the refiner's fire. He will not keep you in the summer heat for one minute longer than what's absolutely necessary. He knows how long your heart needs to soften so that you will hear, accept, release, and bear fruit in the harvest. You can "be ready in and out of season" (2 Timothy 4:2). But first, let me pray for you:

Dear Summer Jesus,

Thank You that just one Word from You can forever change the course of my life. Thank You that I can experience time in two ways. Open my eyes to Your "appointed time," and show me which of the "seasons" I am currently in so that I can hear, accept, release, and bear fruit. I am available to You—even if it means opening myself up to ripen and to possibly being hurt or bruised. Soften my heart. Please don't let me be afraid of the ripening process. Thank You that even though life may feel bro-ken, it is just the beginning. You're not done with me yet! There are still more seasons to come. Amen.

Soul Gardening Questions for Further Reflection

1. Have you ever thought of the physical seasons as spiritually appointed by God? Why or why not? If so, how?

_____

_____

_____

_____

_____

_____

_____

_____

_____

_____

_____

_____

_____

_____

_____

_____

2. Do you currently need more help with standing on
    God's Word, having peace, continuing to ask, or looking
    up to God in this season?

    _____

    _____

    _____

    _____

    _____

    _____

    _____

    _____

    _____

3. Have you ever experienced time in two ways like I did
    when God brought my cat, Lemon, to my doorstep?
    Why or why not? If so, how?

    _____

    _____

    _____

    _____

    _____

    _____

    _____

    _____

    _____

4. How is the Spirit leading you to bear fruit? Is there
    a seed or seeds you are still holding on to that need
    to be released so you can continue on to the next
    spiritual season? Take a few minutes and journal down
    everything you can think of. If it helps, turn back to
    Chapter 2 and re-read all the dreams you wrote down,
    and see if God highlights any one of them that you
    might still be holding on to.

    _____

    _____

    _____

    _____

    _____

    _____

    _____

    _____

    _____

    _____

    _____

    _____

    _____

    _____

    _____

    _____

    _____

    _____

5. Take some time to write your response to the seven
    questions pertaining to a summer spiritual season
    below.

    a. What *pest* continues to plague you?

    _____

    _____

    b. What *theme* is reoccurring in your life right now?

    _____

    _____

    _____

    c. Are there any *Bible verses* that speak life and encour-
        agement into your situation?

    _____

    _____

    _____

    _____

    _____

    _____

    _____

    _____

    _____

    _____

    _____

    _____

d. Have you recently experienced a *miracle*? If so, what was it? How did it make you feel?

_____

_____

_____

_____

e. How are you *feeling* right now?

_____

_____

_____

f. Have you *read* any good books, blogs, or social media posts, or listened to any podcasts?

_____

_____

_____

g. Are there any *songs* that lifted your spirits?

_____

_____

_____

_____

_____

_____

CHAPTER 6

The Harvest is the Word of God {Fall}

"This year's felt like four seasons of winter
And you'd give anything to feel the sun
Always reaching, always climbing
Always second guessing the timing
But God has a plan, a purpose in this
You are His child and don't you forget." (1)

You made it, friend, welcome to fall—the most beautiful season of all! Fall is harvest season. You know this. I know this. Farmers know this. I've struggled the most writing this chapter. Maybe it's because I don't have a miracle to share below. There is no pretty bow to wrap up the four spiritual seasons to say:

Fall is harvest season.

"See? If you do *this* (like I did), then *this* will happen (like it did for me)."

God doesn't work that way. He is not a God in a box. There are no formulas, and I certainly don't want to give that (false) impression in *Soul Gardening: Finding God in Every Season*. What I *do* hope is that through these pages you'll see the importance of cultivating your relationship with God so that He can be found by you in the garden of your soul in every season. That's why I've asked you a lot of questions. Questions, I hope, that motivate you as you explore more of your story while sitting next to Jesus on a garden bench.

You were created for adventure. You are meant to journey on a quest to find God. In winter, I pray He speaks to you personally so that when you plant those dreams as seeds in the dark ground to die in the spring, you can trust the process and be ready for summer while waiting on the fall harvest—even if it doesn't come, is ruined, goes bad, or fails. It reminds me of Habakkuk 3:17-18 that says:

> *You were created for adventure. You are meant to journey on a quest to find God.*

> "Though the fig tree should not blossom,
>   nor fruit be on the vines,
>   the produce of the olive fail
>   and the fields yield no food,
>   the flock be cut off from the fold
>   and there be no herd in the stalls,
>   yet I will rejoice in the Lord;
>   I will take joy in the God of my salvation."

Fall's Miracle

Habakkuk rejoices in God alone. Maybe *that's* the miracle. Over and over God longs to hear thanks and praise not just in the fall season but in *every* season. There is a reason why farmers treasure fall the most. Fall's payday is the culmination of four seasons of hard physical labor. The farmers need to pay bills and hope that what's left will feed their family until the next harvest. Their livelihood depends on it. Sometimes things like bad soil, drought, pests, or a freak storm wreck their best laid plans—and plants. They know they won't be able to plant again until the spring. This is why farmers are always watching the weather and doing everything in their power to prevent a failed harvest...and to safely store up their harvest.

Are your dreams...*treasured in your storehouse?* You might be in a fall spiritual season. If you're unsure of which emotions you may or may not be feeling, turn to the back of the book and find the "What's in Season?" garden party game.

> *Are your dreams treasured in your storehouse? You might be in a fall spiritual season.*

Feel free to mark it up or journal each word that stands out to you that you want to cultivate or eradicate. I'll unpack more of what it means to rest after each harvest in the next chapter, even if the harvest doesn't come or meet your expectations.

Let's make this personal.

What happens if something bad happens to you physically? Maybe you lose your job, get sick, or worse? Or, what happens if something bad happens to you spiritually? Maybe someone else's sin is affecting your harvest, intense spiritual warfare threatens to keep you from God, or maybe He's has asked you to do something and you haven't obeyed *yet*. (Re-read Chapter 5 if you still need help releasing your dreams to God).

I love the quote from Ruth Chou Simons in her book *Beholding and Becoming*. She writes:

"Has staying ahead of the game in all areas of your life become a normal pattern for survival? Have you forgotten that though you're a bound bricklayer by birth you're now a freed child of God through redemption?" (2)

I don't know about you, but no amount of progress in my own life ever seems to reap the kind of harvest that satisfies. Even though I'm a freed child of God, I can't help but continue hustling until the next big thing comes along. That's what makes Haggai 1:6 so interesting. Let's read:

"You have sown much, and harvested little. You eat, but you never have enough; you drink, but you never have your fill. You clothe yourselves, but no one is warm. And he who earns wages does so to put them into a bag with holes."

This verse forever changed my perspective about fall. I wonder if this verse speaks to you, too? Instead of reaping all the hard work and growth from the previous three seasons, I wasn't satisfied. I was focused on my lack, discontent in not becoming a mom yet, and struggling through what felt like an impossible harvest because of current health circumstances.

Please don't give up. Your life is precious. There's a reason God created you, and He's not done with you yet!

I don't know if my confession encourages you, but sometimes the harvest doesn't come in the season you want or in the way you want. Please don't give up. Your life is precious. There's a reason

God created you, and He's not done with you yet! Priscilla Shirer says:

> "Who you are is more important than what you have been called to do." (3)

Who you are is more important than your job title, relationship status, or bank account. Your dreams are valuable even if they have never been written down or planted in the ground—*yet*. You are a treasured vessel waiting to be used by God. God is a gentleman and He will wait patiently for you because He loves you. I know this because He waited on me for many years.

My Story

It took me until my fall spiritual season to understand that I can just read the Bible. I didn't always need my favorite gardening tools every time I spent time with God. That's how I knew my quiet times with God had become a ritual or something to check off each morning. When I read Haggai 1:6, it was in my small travel Bible while on a spiritual retreat to spend time alone with God. Not only did it feel lighter, but I gave myself permission to go away and just spend time with Him. I knew I had become distracted by all the underlines and fun things I added over the past four spiritual seasons in my *Journaling Bible* that made finding God seem like a heavy and difficult burden.

> "We may feel that nothing big or noteworthy happened on our retreat. The benefits of retreating often are not seen until we engage the battle within. Go away and trust God with what happens in your soul." (4)

Thanks to Adele in her *Spiritual Disciplines Handbook*, I was able to get away and ask difficult questions while tending to my soul. It was difficult for me to just *be* with God. I am a dreamer and a doer. It says so in my bio. How about you? How do you spend time with God? Do you desire to just read your Bible and be with Him?

According to Mrs. Calhoun, one of the ways to practice a spiritual retreat is by "detaching from productivity and doing in order to be in the presence of God and attend to his voice alone." (5) She also recommends that you "take only your Bible with you." (6)

So, I did.

I had to be reminded, once again, that God's voice is much softer, slower, and quieter—and requires much patient listening to hear. When I opened to Haggai, I was shocked. I couldn't believe that verse even existed. It's as if the Holy Spirit lifted it off the pages and into my heart. I knew God had found me, because I had just prayed that God would satisfy me. After that spiritual retreat, I felt refreshed to tend to my soul garden in new ways. God taught me how to be satisfied in Him *when* my fall harvest didn't come by feeding me with these five verses below:

⊛ "And you shall eat and be full, and you shall bless the Lord your God for the good land he has given you." (Deuteronomy 8:10)

⊛ "And he will give grass in your fields for your livestock, and you shall eat and be full." (Deuteronomy 11:15)

⊛ "You shall eat in plenty and be satisfied, and praise the name of the Lord your God, who has dealt wondrously with you. And my people shall never again be put to shame." (Joel 2:26)

❀ "But in the fifth year you may eat of its fruit, to increase its yield for you: I am the Lord your God." (Leviticus 19:25)

❀ "Be filled with the Spirit." (Ephesians 5:18b)

These verses encouraged me to start a new journal. I included all the verses that saved my life in previous seasons to remind me that I can just read the Bible. I feasted on the Word, which became like a fire in my mouth (see Jeremiah 5:14; 15:16). I'm so glad I devoured God's precious promises. They helped to satisfy my soul when the harvest didn't come and I experienced a dental crisis that lasted over a year, during which Marc and I moved cross-country *again* during a national pandemic and an unexpected natural disaster.

In my fall spiritual season, I needed to unlock the lesson of how to be satisfied in God alone, and not the harvest—even when it felt like four seasons of winter. I'm so glad I kept feasting on His Word and didn't give up. Maybe that was fall's miracle, but I just couldn't see it yet. Here are the things I did see, however, that helped me through:

❀ *Fall's Pest:* Dissatisfaction

❀ *Fall's Theme:* Thankfulness

❀ *Fall's Key Verses:* Haggai 1:6; Galatians 6:9; Luke 8:11; Deuteronomy 8:3, 10; 11:15; Joel 2:26; Eph. 5:18b; Jeremiah 5:14; 15:16

❀ *Fall's Miracle:* Satisfaction in God Alone

⊛ *Fall's Feeling Words:* Overwhelmed, Fully Ripe, Settled, Labor-Intensive, Present, Sacrifice, Surrender, Feast, Blessed, Thankful, Grateful, Mature, Full, Family, Dream Fulfilled, Homegrown, Growth, Strength, Wonder, Connection, Comfort, Splendor, Promise, Legacy, Flourish Abundance, Long-awaited, Fulfilled, Full, Fruitfulness, Hospitality, Celebrate, Dreamy

⊛ *Fall's Prayer:* "Thank You, Lord. I'm so glad I pressed in—because I *still* want to be healed. My healing can't come in the same season of sowing. I know this now. I ask again in the name of Jesus to wash me in Your blood. Cleanse me from all unrighteousness. I want to be healed. I want to be at peace and in my right mind. Thank You, Lord, for hearing and answering my prayer—for apart from You I can do nothing. Yes and amen."

⊛ *Fall's Book*: *Gideon* by Priscilla Shirer; *Spiritual Disciplines Handbook* by Adele Ahlberg Calhoun

⊛ *Fall's Songs:* "You Are Holy (Prince of Peace)" by Michael W. Smith, "Give Thanks" by Don Moen and Integrity's Hosanna! Music, "Lean Back" (feat. Dion Davis) by Capital City Music, "Make Room" by The Church Will Sing, Elyssa Smith and Community Music, "Open Space" by Housefires, "Known" by Tauren Wells, "Whole Heart (Hold Me Now) – Live" by Hillsong UNITED, "Promises" by Maverick City Music, "Close" (feat. Steven Furtick) by Tauren Wells, "Close - Remix" (feat. Evan & Eris) by Roy Rosh and GIDI, "I'll Give Thanks – Live" by Housefires and

Kirby Kaple, "Perfect Peace" by Tauren Wells, "Slow Down" by Jonathan Ogden

What about you? Do you find yourself growing weary while waiting for the fall harvest? Galatians 6:9 says, "And let us not grow weary of doing good, for in due season we will reap, if we do not give up."

Your Story

The fall harvest brings everybody to the table. It's not a coincidence that we celebrate Thanksgiving during the fall. With plenty of bounty to go around, it's usually easy to give thanks, but what happens if your heart is just as empty as your table? It's easy to pray:

> "Lord, isn't this is the 'due season?' Isn't fall when I should be celebrating the 'appointed time' *of* all the 'great things' You've done for me? If the harvest doesn't come in the fall—then—*when*?"

I know what you're thinking because I thought the same thing, too. The harvest is the Word of God. This is the sixth spiritual principle of soul gardening. I had to learn how to feast on His Word like the Israelites did in the desert, and maybe—just maybe—you're currently learning how to do the same. Here's a verse that Moses used to remind the Israelites of this spiritual principle. Let's read:

> "'And he humbled you and let you hunger and fed you with manna, which you did not know, nor did your fathers know, that he might make you know that man does not live by bread alone, but man lives by every word that comes from the mouth of the Lord.'"
>
> (Deuteronomy 8:3)

The harvest is the
Word of God. This is
the sixth spiritual principle
of soul gardening.

This verse is a great reminder of why you and I must feast on "every word that comes from the mouth of the Lord." Did you know that when Jesus was in the wilderness, He quoted this same passage from Deuteronomy when He was tempted by Satan? Fun fact: Jesus directly quoted Deuteronomy during *all* three temptations.

It can be hard to meet temptation with Scripture when the dreams you planted in the previous season haven't come to fruition—*yet*. Every time you are tempted, like Jesus, ask God for the strength to find satisfaction in Him and His Word alone. Each time you use a Word against Satan you are planting a seed. This is because, "The seed is the word of God" (Luke 8:11).

> *You can trust that each seed planted will bear fruit for His kingdom because Jesus is Lord of the harvest. Without Him, the harvest isn't possible.*

You can trust that each seed planted will bear fruit for His kingdom because Jesus is Lord of the harvest. Without Him, the harvest isn't possible. This is a not only a promise for you and for me, but a sure foundation to stand on when all fails—including the harvest. But first, let me pray for you:

Dear Fall Jesus,

I confess I'm struggling. It's easy for me to pray to be satisfied in You, but another thing to completely trust and make room in my heart for You. Forgive me when I fill up every place in me that should be filled with You. Give me the desire to read and feast on Your Word. Holy

Spirit, fill me with You so that I am not tempted by all the things I think I want or even need right this minute. Help me to see that even if the harvest doesn't come, or feels impossible, nothing is impossible with You. You are God and You do not lie. Keep my heart tender and looking to You for more instead of draining those around me to give me something that only You can fill. Help me to keep looking to You alone instead of people, places, and things—including the weather that can easily distract. Amen.

Soul Gardening Questions for Further Reflection

1. Have you ever felt abandoned by God in an hour or season of deepest need? How did you feel and what did you do to make it through?

    _____

    _____

    _____

    _____

    _____

    _____

    _____

    _____

    _____

2. Do you struggle more with *being* or *doing*? Why?

_____

_____

_____

_____

_____

_____

_____

_____

_____

_____

3. Whether it's being content to just read your Bible
    or changing up the gardening tools you're currently
    using, what is one way you'd like to experience God's
    presence in a new and fresh way this season?

_____

_____

_____

_____

_____

_____

_____

_____

_____

4. Have you experienced a time in your life when you
    weren't satisfied with God? What did you do to
    overcome it?

    _____

    _____

    _____

    _____

    _____

    _____

    _____

    _____

5. Take some time to write your response to the seven
    questions pertaining to a fall spiritual season below.
    Going forward, I hope these same seven questions
    throughout each spiritual season have helped you to
    discover which season you are currently in so you can
    be encouraged to find God in *every* season.

    a. What *pest* continues to plague you?

    _____

    _____

    _____

    b. What *theme* is reoccurring in your life right now?

    _____

    _____

    _____

c. Are there any *Bible verses* that speak life and encouragement into your situation?

_____

_____

_____

_____

_____

_____

_____

_____

_____

_____

d. Have you recently experienced a *miracle*? If so, what was it? How did it make you feel?

_____

_____

_____

_____

_____

_____

_____

_____

e. How are you *feeling* right now?

_____

_____

_____

f. Have you *read* any good books, blogs, or social media posts, or listened to any podcasts?

_____

_____

_____

_____

_____

_____

_____

g. Are there any *songs* that lifted your spirits?

_____

_____

_____

_____

_____

_____

_____

SECTION III

Find Peace for Your Soul

CHAPTER 7

After Each Harvest...Rest

> "And on the eighth day, God looked down
> on his planned paradise and said, 'I need
> a caretaker.' So God made a farmer." (1)

After each harvest...rest. This is the seventh and final spiritual principle of soul gardening. I can write this with confidence for two reasons. The first is that God rested with His creation on the seventh day (see Genesis 2:1-3). The second is that God commanded the Israelites to rest every seven days and keep it holy (see Exodus 20:8). God didn't just rest with His creation one time, but He commanded a Sabbath one day a week to help us slow down and spend time with Him.

If you look at the seasons, they follow a similar pattern of work and rest. Winter is *that* season; it is a season of rest. I know it's hard to imagine if you don't live in an area where there are four seasons. I'm grateful that our second cross-country move brought Marc and me to the Midwest where I could finally experience the four seasons, including my first real winter as an adult. It also gave me the inspiration to finish *Soul Gardening: Finding God in Every Season*.

I don't know about you, but I feel better physically and spiritually when I take time to rest—and not just on a Saturday or Sunday. So why, then, is it so hard to find peace for the soul? Here are two examples from Scripture to help you see why rest is difficult, hurts, or feels impossible—like slamming into a brick wall after a busy season.

1. *You are unwilling.* Isaiah 30:15 says: "For thus said the Lord God, the Holy One of Israel, 'In returning and rest you shall be saved; in quietness and in trust shall be your strength.' But you were unwilling."

2. *God is disciplining you.* Hebrews 12:11-13 (*emphasis added*) says: "For the moment all discipline seems painful rather than pleasant, but later it yields the *peaceful* fruit of righteousness to those who have been trained by it. Therefore lift your drooping hands and strengthen your weak knees, and make straight paths for your feet, so that what is lame may not be put out of joint but rather be healed."

God used this verse to drive home a seed He had already planted in my heart fifteen years prior. I didn't believe peace would ever be possible because I have anxiety (Generalized Anxiety Disorder or GAD). While worshipping on the piano, God teasingly whispered, "I did it!" I knew what He meant because I had begun to experience feelings of peace for the first time ever.

It wasn't until I was on vacation visiting the Ft. Worth Botanic Garden with Marc that I found my name on a card in the gift shop that said, "Peaceful." You know those name cards that have your name and the meaning of your name? I immediately bought it and put it in my journal as a reminder that God was helping me find peace for my soul. He was *literally* meeting me in the garden. I don't know about you, but I believe in signs.

I'm so glad I held on to God's still, small voice and that sign at the garden, because it wasn't until my fall spiritual season that I had to put into practice what I had learned about peace when the harvest I wanted didn't happen.

After each harvest...rest.
This is the seventh
and final spiritual principle
of soul gardening.

God's discipline is painful. He had to realign my dreams and the expectation of those dreams to His "appointed time." I almost missed verse 13 that says to "lift," "strengthen," and "make straight paths" so that God could bring me peace and heal me. I had to trust that His promises would come at the "appointed time."

> *I don't know what will bring you rest after the harvest season, but I know you can choose to be thankful no matter the outcome—because peace is possible in every season. I know because my soul has experienced it, too!*

Your name doesn't have to mean "peaceful" for God to give you peace for your soul. In fact, Jesus says, "Peace I leave with you; my peace I give to you. Not as the world gives do I give to you. Let not your hearts be troubled, neither let them be afraid" (John 14:27). I don't know what will bring you rest after the harvest season, but I know you can choose to be thankful no matter the outcome—because peace is possible in every season. I know because my soul has experienced it, too!

Peace for your soul comes from God. Paul encourages us when we become anxious. He writes:

> "Do not be anxious about anything, but in everything by prayer and supplication with thanksgiving let your requests be made known to God. And the peace of God, which surpasses all understanding, will guard your hearts and your minds in Christ Jesus." (Philippians 4:6-7)

God needs to expose false beliefs about fear in the fall season.

> "Fear and peace stand in opposition. We cannot experience God's peace if we are dwelling in fear, and, on the other side of the coin, we will not dwell on fear if we are experiencing God's peace. Fear and peace do not live together." (2)

A peaceful harvest is possible for the soul because it is a fruit of wisdom that Jesus gives. Another verse to support this is:

> "But the wisdom from above is first pure, then peaceable, gentle, open to reason, full of mercy and good fruits, impartial and sincere. And a harvest of righteousness is sown in peace by those who make peace." (James 3:17-18)

A peaceful harvest is possible for the soul because it is a fruit of wisdom that Jesus gives.

Do you believe this? I hope you do! You are an overcomer! Jesus says:

> "I have said these things to you, that in me you may have peace. In the world you will have tribulation. But take heart; I have overcome the world." (John 16:33)

I know I just threw out a bunch of Scriptures, however, *Soul Gardening* is my way of showing you through word *and* action that peace for your soul is possible even when your fall harvest doesn't come or you feel the current season doesn't

You are an overcomer!

tell your story. *Soul Gardening* is also my restoration story through the lens of nature while learning how to dream in a garden and to discover my spiritual season, which is how God finally brought peace to my soul. I hope that by planting your own soul garden that *you* will find peace, too!

> "Every breath I breathe an invitation
> To believe You are creating
> Something good
> Though this season doesn't tell my story
> I know You'll move mountains for me
> You're just that good
> So I'll give thanks to God
> When I don't have enough
> 'Cause He's more than enough
> And He knows what I need." (3)

Encountering the Lord of Hosts:

In my fall spiritual season, when everything was crumbling around me, God set me up for the biggest reveal ever. I discovered the Lord of hosts waiting for me. He revealed His character and His name to me while studying the book of Jeremiah. I asked God to help me have a better understanding of the Lord of hosts.

> "The name [the Lord of hosts] is used to remind us of who our God really is: the powerful Commander in Chief with all of the angels at His disposal. Our problems are not too big for Him. He is holy, sovereign,

and able to do what He says He will do...Do you want to know Him better? He wants to know you! He wants you to ask Him questions and wait in His presence for answers." (4)

When I asked God, He showed me that very same day! The Lord of hosts plants and gives life, plucks up and destroys. He is *both/and*. The whole time I was studying the seasons and walking with God in my soul garden, I didn't

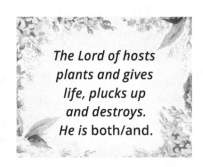

The Lord of hosts plants and gives life, plucks up and destroys. He is both/and.

know Whom or what aspect of His character I was so drawn to. Now I know because I have encountered Him. I called upon the Lord of hosts who has the power to plant and pluck up, build and destroy. Next, I discovered that Hannah was the first person in the Bible to ever call upon the Lord of hosts. Let's read:

> "[Hannah] was deeply distressed and prayed to the Lord and wept bitterly. And she vowed a vow and said, 'O Lord of hosts, if you will indeed look on the affliction of your servant and remember me and not forget your servant, but will give to your servant a son, then I will give him to the Lord all the days of his life, and no razor shall touch his head.'" (1 Samuel 1:10-11)

You see?

It's like I just learned the name of my best friend, the Lord of hosts. The God who was my personal tour guide in the gardens I visited showed up in *my* own soul garden, inviting me into a new and deeper journey with Him. Not only that, but I discovered His power to give life to the barren.

When I prayed that same prayer of Hannah, I was a hot mess. A total wreck. Wouldn't you know—one month after I prayed to the Lord of hosts and asked God for a child, Marc and I found out we were having a baby?! Not only did the Lord of hosts keep me alive, but He restored my health and planted new life in my womb. But it wasn't during the fall spiritual season I hoped it would be in. It was actually while living in the Midwest during our first adult winter, exactly four years, ten months, and fourteen days from the day God promised me we would have children to the day we found out we were pregnant again.

Naming and discovering the seasons was all a labor of love to heal from the hurt of my miscarriage. I know that now.

I was absolutely shocked that life can happen in total darkness, but I shouldn't be surprised, because each seed needs to die in order to sprout (see Chapter 3). It was the six years of waiting since a heartbreaking miscarriage that caused me to become a prisoner of hope (see Zechariah 9:12). Some days I believed; others I did not.

Now I know that the Lord of hosts is not only the God behind the four spiritual seasons, but the One who gives life. He is the One who is inviting you and me into the garden to continue to give new life to our souls.

From my first spiritual season in 2016 until 2021, I was trying to make sense of God's promises. I hurt because my circumstances hurt. Moving to Iowa exposed my shame, and then the Lord of hosts removed it. He freed me, but not the way I hoped, expected—or demanded. I needed to trust in God and His timing. In the middle of my quest, God gave

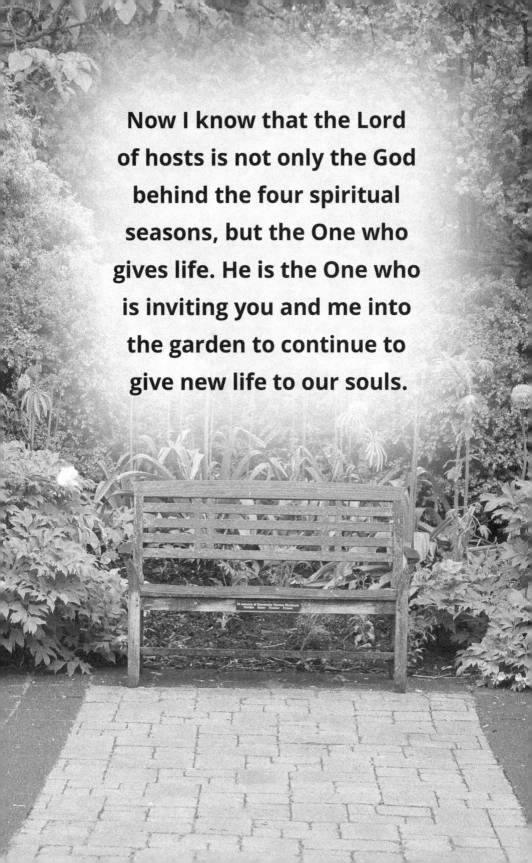

Now I know that the Lord of hosts is not only the God behind the four spiritual seasons, but the One who gives life. He is the One who is inviting you and me into the garden to continue to give new life to our souls.

me a prophetic word on seasons, changed my name, and revealed His name to me as the Lord of hosts. Naming and discovering the seasons was all a labor of love to heal from the hurt of my miscarriage. I know that now.

Whom Did You Encounter?

What about you? Whom have you encountered in your soul garden? No two soul gardens are alike so I wouldn't be surprised if you met a different aspect of God's character. I would love to know more of your journey while reading *Soul Gardening*. I'd also love to know more of your story and who the Lord revealed Himself to you as. I hope you'll email me at renee@reneefisher.com and share your *Soul Gardening* journey.

It's been a pleasure to be your host, but for now I think it's best to let the real garden host take over. You're in good hands, and I'm sure the Lord of hosts is already there waiting like He was for me, too! He's saved you a seat, and you don't need an invitation!

> "Quiet my soul 'cause You're teaching me how to slow down
>
> Surrender it all, let You take control and slow down I know You're not far away from me, You are so close now
>
> I'm waiting in the stillness, I need to hear Your voice now." (5)

Soul Gardening **Questions for Further Reflection**

1. Is there a miracle you are dreaming and waiting on God to cultivate from seed to sprout to harvest...and beyond?

   _____

   _____

   _____

   _____

   _____

   _____

   _____

   _____

   _____

   _____

2. What did you learn from dreaming in a garden?

   _____

   _____

   _____

   _____

   _____

   _____

   _____

   _____

3. Do you know which spiritual season you're in now?

_____

_____

_____

_____

4. Whom have you encountered in your soul garden?
    Did you find God's peace?

_____

_____

_____

_____

_____

_____

_____

_____

_____

_____

The Final Feast

> "Then, at last, the Spirit's work will
> reach harvest time, and God will be
> all in all (1 Cor. 15:28). With this in view,
> both the Spirit and the Bride say, 'Come!'
> (Rev. 22:17)." (1)

No one ever told me about a lexicon. I knew about a Bible concordance and an interlinear Bible, but never the lexicon. I was more than halfway through Trinity Seminary to get my Master of Arts in Bible and Theology when a friend, Brenda Stroth, told me about the lexicon and showed me how to use one. (Crazy that I never heard about it through my studies!) Let me explain:

- ❈ *A Bible concordance* shows you similar verses with the same Old Testament Hebrew or New Testament Greek word found in a particular passage.

If you go to BibleGateway.com and look up all of the verses in the Bible that mention "peace" or whatever word you are interested studying, it will show you a neat and organized list of all of the mentions of "peace" in the Bible. For instance, when I looked up the Greek word for "peaceful" in Hebrews 12:11, I discovered a variation of my name, Renee. Now I know why I found that name card at the Ft. Worth Botanic Garden. My name, Renee, really does mean "peaceful"!

⊛ *An interlinear Bible* shows you the meaning of an Old
Testament Hebrew or New Testament Greek word—
not the English meaning but the original Hebrew or
Greek meaning, which can sometimes provide more
shades of meaning.

If you go to https://www.biblestudytools.com/interlin-
ear-bible/ and look up the original meaning of a word found
in the Bible, you will find what that particular word means in
Hebrew or Greek. For instance, when I looked up the phrase
"appointed time" found in Psalm 102:13 and discovered the
Hebrew word meant "seasons," that started me on my quest,
which has led to me writing *Soul Gardening*. That's how deep
and penetrating the Word is. Just *one* Hebrew word changed
my entire life forever!

⊛ *A lexicon* shows you the meaning of the root word
from the original Old Testament Hebrew or New
Testament Greek word.

If you go to https://www.blueletterbible.org/ and look
up the verse in the Interlinear Bible to find the Hebrew or
Greek word, then you can click on the root word (etymol-
ogy), if there is one, to find even more shades of meaning.
For instance, while Brenda was teaching me how to use this
free tool, I told her that I had been prayerfully chewing on
one Hebrew word, *mô'ēḏ*, which means "appointed time"
or "seasons," for over four years. It wasn't until I had the
missing link of the lexicon that I learned that the root word
of *mô'ēḏ* is *yā'aḏ*, which means "espoused" or "feast." (2) This
helped me connect the dots from Genesis 1:14 to Revelation
19:9. God created the "seasons" in Genesis 1:14, which also
means "appointed time," *and* now we know the root word of

"seasons" means "feast." Putting these two together, we see that the final "feast" in Revelations 19:9 is with Jesus as His "espoused" in the marriage supper of the Lamb.

I share about "the final feast" in the epilogue because God is still showing shades of meaning as I continue to study His Word. It has been an honor and pleasure to chew on the Hebrew word for "seasons" since 2017, and the fact that He is still speaking to me just shows you how powerful one Bible verse can be—even one word in one Bible verse! My mind is *still* blown and words cannot describe how this one Hebrew word has forever changed my life. I can't wait for the day when I get to celebrate the final feast with God as His bride, as well as spend eternity with Him!

What about you?

- Is there any verse in the Bible that you'd like to know if there are more similar verses on the same topic? Start with the Bible concordance on BibleGateway.com.

- Is there a particular word from a particular verse that captured your attention that you want to look up? Start with BibleStudyTools.org and click on the Interlinear Bible.

- Is there a particular Hebrew or Greek word you'd like to learn more about, particularly its root and origins along with the meaning? Go to BibleStudyTools.com and start your search!

Thanks for letting me put on my seminary hat for a moment to equip you with three more gardening tools:

1. *Bible concordance:* Cultivates...studying the Word and looking up similar verses that share a specific word or phrase.

2. *Interlinear Bible:* Cultivates...studying the Word while learning the basic Hebrew and Greek of a particular word found within a Bible verse to better understand the shades of meaning found within the Word of God.

3. *Lexicon:* Cultivates...studying the Word while diving deeper into the Hebrew and Greek of a particular word found within a Bible verse to better understand the shades of meaning found within the Word of God.

Happy *Soul Gardening* to you, friend. May you find peace for your soul as your garden grows. Thanks for giving me the pleasure of being your garden tour guide. Please to go my website ReneeFisher.com and register for the next online and/or in person garden party, as well as the free PDF version of the garden party games found in the next several pages. And finally, thanks for entrusting me with your story for His glory. I hope to meet you online or in person soon!

Your Dream Defender,

Renee Fisher

Garden Party Games

Unlock Your Spiritual Season

You cannot miss your "appointed time" if you are a believer in Jesus Christ. No matter what season of life you find yourself in, you can answer these seven questions below to help you unlock your current spiritual season. It is my hope that as you take the time to answer the questions below, you'll uncover your secret key to unlock your garden where you can dream with God and discover your spiritual season.

1. What *pest* continues to plague you?

2. What *theme* is reoccurring in your life right now?

3. Are there any *Bible verses* that speak life and encouragement into your situation?

4. Have you recently experienced a *miracle*? If so, what was it? How did it make you feel?

5. How are you *feeling* right now?

6. Have you *read* any good books, blogs, or social media posts, or listened to any podcasts?

7. Are there any *songs* that lifted your spirits?

What's in Season?

> "In fact, it's in the imperfect—the dirt— where things grow. Not despite the mess and tension, but right smack in the middle of it." (1)

Circle words you want to cultivate and cross out the words you want to eradicate *this* season. I highly recommend doing this exercise *every* season to help you see where you've grown and what areas you're still cultivating or eradicating.

CULTIVATE

Acceptance	Calm	Deliberate
Adventure	Caring	Delight
Alive	Carefree	Devotion
Amazed	Capable	Driven
Ambitious	Cautious	Efficiency
Analyzer	Cheerful	Empathy
Appreciative	Chosen	Encouragement
Approved	Close	Energized
Assertive	Comfort	Ethical
Astonished	Confidence	Excitement
Aware	Consideration	Expectancy
Balanced	Content	Faith
Beautiful	Creativity	Fascination
Blissful	Curious	Fearless
Brave	Deep	Forgiveness

Freedom

Friendly

Full

Funny

Generosity

Genuine

Gentleness

Good Listener

Goodness

Gratefulness

Growth

Happiness

Harmony

Health

Helpfulness

Honor

Hope

Hospitality

Humility

Helping

Imagination

Independence

Innocence

Inspiration

Inquisitive

Joy

Justice

Kindness

Leadership

Light

Love

Loyal

Meditation

Mischievous

Natural

Nurturing

Obedience

Open

Optimistic

Organized

Passionate

Patience

Peace

Playful

Power

Purity

Purpose

Quiet

Real

Refined

Relaxed

Reliable

Resilience

Responsible

Restoration

Revolutionary

Righteous

Self-Assurance

Self-Control

Satisfied, Serene

Silence

Silly

Simplicity

Sincere

Smart

Sobriety

Soft

Solitude

Sparkling

Spontaneous

Stability

Strength

Supportive

Surprised

Sweet

Tenderness

Thoughtfulness

Tickled

Tolerance

Trust

Understanding

Usefulness

Vivaciousness

Vulnerable

Warm

Whimsical

Whole

Willing

Wishful

Wonder

Worth

ERADICATE

Abandonment

Accusation

Afraid

Agitation

Aggressive

Aggravation

Alarmed

Alone

Anger

Anguish

Annoyed

Anxious

Apathetic

Asleep

Attacked

Beaten

Betrayed

Bitterness

Blah

Boredom

Broken

Bruised

Bullied

Burdened

Burnt-out

Callousness

Carelessness

Cheated

Coerced

Cold

Complacent

Condemned

Conflicted

Confused

Consumed

Controlling

Critical

Crushed

Deceiving

Defeated

Depressed

Desperation

Disobedience

Disorganized

Dull

Envy

Exhaustion

Exploitation

Failure

Fake

Fearful

Flaky

Foolishness

Forcefulness

Heartless

Homesick

Hopeless

Hostility

Humiliation

Hurt

Hyper-Sensitive

Hysterical

Idiotic

Ignorance

Impatience

Impulsivity

Inadequate

Incapable

Incompetence

Indecisiveness

Indifference

Inferiority

Insecurity

Insensitivity

Irresponsibility

Irritation

Isolation

Jaded

Jealous

Judged

Laziness

Lonely

Mean

Needy

Neglectful

Obsessiveness

Outrage

Overwhelmed

Paralyzed

Pessimism

Predictability

Procrastination

Pushy

Regret	Skepticism	Unsafe
Rejection	Sloppiness	Unloved
Reluctance	Spiteful	Unwelcome
Resistance	Stuck	Used
Revenge	Superficiality	Useless
Rebellion	Suspicious	Victimized
Recklessness	Tense	Violated
Rough	Threatened	Violent
Rude	Tight	Volatile
Sadness	Trapped	Weak
Scared	Tricked	Wishy-Washy
Self-Centered	Unappreciated	Workaholic
Selfishness	Uncomfortable	Worry
Shame	Uninvolved	Wounded

Were you surprised by any of the words you circled or crossed out? What word(s) do you hope to cultivate this season?

_____

_____

_____

_____

_____

_____

_____

_____

_____

_____

_____

_____

Create Your Own Scripture Garden

"Where flowers bloom so does hope." (1)

In *Soul Gardening,* I hope you discovered Jesus in your soul garden. I hope you know by now that you can find God in *every* season. I also hope the gardening tools shared in Chapter 1 were helpful to cultivate the soil of your soul, which is now your foundation for all future growth. One of the ways to grow your soul garden is by starting a Scripture Garden. I got this idea from the Denver Botanical Garden. They had a sign that said Scripture Garden, and in this little garden they had all these religious symbols and plants that represented soul growth. I took a picture and knew I'd use this term to encourage others, including myself, by planting my own Scripture Garden.

One of the ways to grow your soul garden is by starting a Scripture Garden.

To create your own Scripture Garden, you'll need good soil, which is *you*! You are the soul who hears the word, accepts it, and bears fruit for His kingdom. God wants to meet with you personally and speak directly to the very thing that threatens to keep you from Him. Don't forget that every fear can be traced back to a lie you are believing to be true, and remember there *is* a verse in the Bible just for you and your current situation. Grab your journal and make a list of all the verses that encourage and challenge you—especially ones that you feel are a promise from God.

> "For the word of God is living and active, sharper than any two-edged sword, piercing to the division of soul and of spirit, of joints and of marrow, and discerning the thoughts and intentions of the heart." (Hebrews 4:12)

I've given you space below to plant your Scripture Garden. I've also shared mine (well, just the date I planted each garden bed with scriptures I continue to cultivate to this day). If you're not sure where to start, pick a couple of verses found in this book or spend some time on BibleGateway.com searching for your favorite Bible verses if you don't know the references. (I do this all the time).

Take your time to remember what seeds you planted in previous seasons that you are still waiting to see grow. Write these verses below. This is a legacy project and not something you will complete overnight. I hope to pass this down to my children.

Once you've written down all the verses that you can think of, begin feasting on the Word! You never know when you'll need to eat your Scripture Garden. Save it for a rainy day or for a difficult season. Consider buying a keepsake journal for your new Scripture Garden or get creative by making a collage or putting them on an app in your phone so they are easily accessible. I bought a cheap hot pink journal from the grocery store and organized the verses into sections that represent different times in my life. For instance, my Scripture Garden includes garden beds that I have organized into themes and dates, which are:

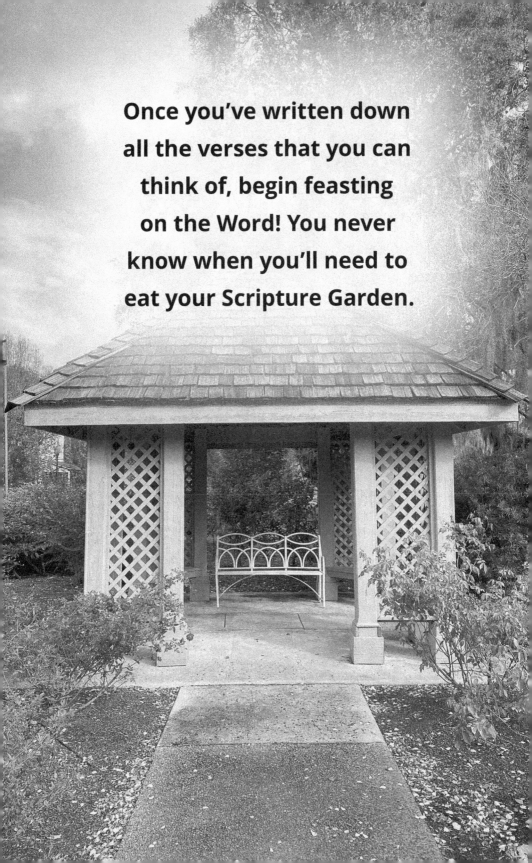

Once you've written down all the verses that you can think of, begin feasting on the Word! You never know when you'll need to eat your Scripture Garden.

1. Overcoming Fear - Planted 1993

2. Overcoming Temptation & the Spiritual Battle - Planted 1993

3. Promise for a Future Husband - Planted 1998/ Harvested in 2011

4. Promise for Healing - Planted 1998

5. Promise for Ministry - Planted 2003

6. Cultivating Life and Fruitfulness - Planted 2007

7. Prayers for Marriage with Marc - Planted 2011

8. Promise for Future Family - Planted 2016/Harvested in 2021

9. God of Refuge - Planted 2016/Harvested in 2020

10. Hearing the Holy Spirit - Planted in 2016

11. Cultivating Seasons and Dreams - Planted in 2016

12. God's Discipline, a "Peaceful" Harvest - Planted 2019

13. The Indwelling Presence - Planted 2020

14. Devouring the Word - Planted 2020

I have a confession to make. I wouldn't have made it through my difficult fall spiritual season without my Scripture Garden. There were days I only had energy to read a few of these verses at a time and meditate on them. Eventually, as with each difficult season, it passed, and I'm grateful to have a record of every verse that saved my life, because "man lives by every word that comes from the mouth of the Lord" (Deuteronomy 8:3b).

Please use the spaces below to write down your favorite Bible verses. Then, when you're ready, you can organize them into themed garden beds and assign the year you planted them! What a great way to begin cultivating the faithfulness of God and to meet with the Lord of hosts on the garden bench.

I have a confession to make. I wouldn't have made it through my difficult fall spiritual season without my Scripture Garden.

_____

_____

_____

_____

_____

_____

_____

_____

_____

_____

_____

_____

_____

_____

_____

_____

_____

_____

_____

Soul Gardening Quotes

I would love it if you would share your favorite quotes from *Soul Gardening*. I made it easier to share by picking my favorite quotes from the book below. Please feel free to pick from the hashtags below when you share. #SoulGardeningBook #ReneeFisher #AmReading #AlwaysTendYourSoulGarden

The Seven Spiritual Principles of *Soul Gardening* are:

1. Every Garden Starts with Good Soil
2. Each Dream is a Seed Waiting to Be Planted
3. Each Seed is Planted in the Dark
4. You Cannot Sow and Harvest in the Same Season
5. Ripe Fruit Bruises Easily
6. The Harvest is the Word of God
7. After Each Harvest...Rest

Which Spiritual Season Are You In?

1. Are your dreams...*waiting for the right time*? You might be in a winter spiritual season.

2. Are your dreams...*preparing to sprout*? You might be in a spring spiritual season.

3. Are your dreams...*ready for harvest*? You might be in a summer spiritual season.

4. Are your dreams....*treasured in your storehouse*? You might be in a fall spiritual season.

Life began in a garden.

Grow slow.

Let nature nurture your soul. Let's dream together while learning from the rhythms of the seasons.

Always tend your soul garden.

You and I were both planted and *planned* by God to do good works before we were born.

God wants to meet with you personally and speak directly to the very thing that threatens to keep you from Him.

A seed planted is not hidden. Every seed needs to die before it sprouts.

Forgiveness is not the end of your story—or mine. After death comes life!

Dream deep and wide because your soul is the center where dreams awaken. It's up to you to open up your heart to God and His dreams for you.

Give yourself permission to dream. It's okay to dream slow. Nature doesn't rush and neither should you.

To dream is to live!

Our dreams are important to Him. Your dreams don't work unless He does!

If you're not afraid of your dreams—your dreams are too small! That's why you walk by faith and *not* by feelings alone.

No two seasons are the same. It's the same with spiritual seasons. Some winters are colder and more intense than others. That's what faith is for!

It is usually when you are spiritually or physically exhausted that you are most vulnerable for physical burnout and a spiritual attack.

Sometimes the very season that threatens your life becomes *the* door into the divine presence of God, to hear His voice and receive what you need for the journey ahead.

God doesn't need you to do "great things" for Him and His kingdom. It's actually the other way around.

The one thing that can cure and heal you is often the one thing you fear most.

You can tell whether your healing is from God if it brings freedom and healing. If it doesn't— chances are it's not from Him.

Oftentimes when God speaks a word, you don't see its manifestation right away.

I believe God's promises are not a result of something you'll do but something He will do for you.

If God speaks a word—it *will* happen. I don't want you to pray for something God hasn't promised.

Seasons are divine, and they each have their "appointed time."

As long as earth exists, "seedtime and harvest, cold and heat, summer and winter, day and night, shall not cease" (Genesis 8:22).

God imprinted a divine order of the four seasons in nature so you can trust in Him and His "appointed time" in your life.

When I was afraid, God renewed my soul and set me back on the path to discovering my spiritual season. I believe He wants to do this for you, too.

You can't miss your "appointed time" because God created the "seasons," and He's in charge. The harvest belongs to Him.

Let the seed go, friend.

You *are* ripening, friend! You just may not know it yet. Don't be surprised if your bruises begin multiplying as the fruit of Spirit exponentially increases in you, making you more like Him.

You were created for adventure. You are meant to journey on a quest to find God.

Please don't give up. Your life is precious. There's a reason God created you, and He's not done with you yet!

You can trust that each seed planted will bear fruit for His kingdom because Jesus is Lord of the harvest. Without Him, the harvest isn't possible.

I don't know what will bring you rest after the harvest season, but I know you can choose to be thankful no matter the outcome—because peace *is* possible in every season. I know because my soul has experienced it, too!

You are an overcomer!

The Lord of hosts plants and gives life, plucks up and destroys. He is *both/and*. He is not only the God behind the four spiritual seasons but the One who gives life. He is the One who is inviting you and me into the garden to continue to give new life to our souls.

If there's one thing I know and now remember—seasons are divine, and they each have their "appointed time." You and I cannot miss our "appointed time." This is the best news ever!

Acknowledgments

All glory, honor, thanks, and praise to the Lord of hosts for meeting with me in the garden and waiting for me there. Thank You for finding me. I want to be found in You—for all time!

Thanks to my husband, Marc, who is my best friend and adventure buddy. It was your suggestion to visit the New York Botanical Garden that sparked my love for gardens and the PeacefulFisher.com project. What would I do without you? Thank you for being my amazing husband.

Thanks to my writing buddy, Starfish, for always being by my side and encouraging me when I needed to take a walk or a nap.

Thanks to my parents for being my number one fans and reading everything I write, and for your praise, feedback, and edits.

Thanks to my beta book group readers, Caite Balderas and Rebecca Polanco, for your support, friendship, and prayers—including feedback to help me finish strong.

Thanks to my wonderful editor, Rebekah Benham, for being by my side from my first book, *Faithbook of Jesus*, to my most recent book *Soul Gardening*, which is hopefully not my last. I value your friendship, as well as professional expertise as an editor. I love that I can trust you with my heart on paper, as well as the many clients I send your way.

Thanks to Nelly Murariu, my pink-haired and very creative graphic designer, who has been pure joy to work with since redoing the cover for my book, *Forgiving Others, Forgiving Me.* Your book cover and interior book designs are priceless. It was actually your design for a client that became the creative spark to finishing *Soul Gardening,* because I could finally picture my book and the cover! God has given you a gift, my friend, and it is a wonderful thing to behold!

Thanks to all my friends, family, and clients who have cheered me on since I first released that prophetic word on the seasons on my blog in 2017. If there's one thing I know and now remember, seasons are divine, and they each have their "appointed time." You and I cannot miss our "appointed time." This is the best news ever!

About the Author

Renee Fisher is a dreamer and a doer. She is a spirit-led worshipper, author, photographer, and coach. She is passionate about defending dreams and spurring others forward to love and good deeds (Hebrews 10:24). #DreamDefender

Renee is a BIG fan of glitter and gardens. She is a graduate of Biola University and resides in the Midwest where she experiences all four seasons with her amazing family. Connect at ReneeFisher.com and PeacefulFisher.com.

Notes

Letter to the Reader

(1) Bruce Corley, Steve W. Lemke, and Grant I. Lovejoy, *Biblical Hermeneutics* (Nashville, TN: B&H Publishing Group, 2002), 313.

(2) Nancy Guthrie, *Even Better Than Eden: Nine Ways the Bible's Story Changes Everything about Your Story* (Wheaton, IL: Crossway, 2018), 24.

Introduction: Garden Party Invitation

(1) *Goodreads*, s.v. "Eleanor Roosevelt," accessed May 25, 2021, https://www.goodreads.com/quotes/6358-the-future-belongs-to-those-who-believe-in-the-beauty.

Chapter 1

(1) Sarah Beth Marr, *Whispers and Wildflowers: 30 Days to Slow Your Pace, Savor Scripture & Draw Closer to God* (Grand Rapids, MI: Baker Books, 2019), 102.

(2) Edith Schaeffer, *Hidden Art* (Wheaton, IL: Tyndale House Publishers, 1971), 23.

(3) Nancy Guthrie, *Even Better Than Eden: Nine Ways the Bible's Story Changes Everything about Your Story* (Wheaton, IL: Crossway, 2018), 12.

(4) Ibid.

(5) Maria Furlough, *Breaking the Fear Cycle: How to Find Peace for Your Anxious Heart* (Grand Rapids, MI: Revell, 2018), 37.

Chapter 2

(1) *Goodreads*, s.v. "Audrey Hepburn," accessed May 24, 2021, https://www.goodreads.com/quotes/831377-to-plant-a-garden-is-to-believe-in-tomorrow.

(2) Walter Bruggemann, *The Prophetic Imagination* (Minneapolis, MN: Fortress Press, 2001), 110.

(3) *Bible Study Tools*, s.v. "Chalam," accessed June 28, 2017, http://www.biblestudytools.com/lexicons/hebrew/kjv/chalam.html.

(4) *Henry Matisse Quotes,* s.v. "There will always be flowers for those who want to see them," accessed July 7, 2017, https://www.henrimatisse.org/henri-matisse-quotes.jsp.

(5) *MetroLyrics*, s.v. "Chris Renzema - Springtime Lyrics," https://www.metrolyrics.com/springtime-lyrics-chris-renzema.html.

(6) Ruth Haley Barton, *Invitation to Solitude and Silence: Experiencing God's Transforming Presence* (Downers Grove, IL: IVP Books, 2010), 67.

(7) Leeana Tankersley, *Brazen: The Courage to Find the You That's Been Hiding* (Grand Rapids, MI: Revell, 2016), 19.

Chapter 3

(1) Josephine Nuese, The Country Garden (NY: New York, Scribners, 1970), 3.

(2) Jen Wilkin, *None Like Him: 10 Ways God is Different from Us (and Why That's a Good Thing)* (Wheaton, IL: Crossway, 2016), 24.

(3) Ruth Haley Barton, *Invitation to Solitude and Silence: Experiencing God's Transforming Presence* (Downers Grove, IL: IVP Books, 2010), 76.

(4) Ibid, 31.

(5) Ibid, 86.

(6) Ibid, 90.

Chapter 4

(1) *Spotify*, s.v. "Saints Church - The Roar of the Rain," accessed May 22, 2017, https://open.spotify.com/episode/5frNKU4Zy5esPJKH8f2vfE?si=LG53ibaYQl-y7iuC-Tm1nA.

(2) Maria Furlough, *Breaking the Fear Cycle: How to Find Peace for Your Anxious Heart* (Grand Rapids, MI: Revell, 2018), 87.

(3) *Spotify*, s.v. "Saints Church - The Roar of the Rain," accessed May 22, 2017, https://open.spotify.com/episode/5frNKU4Zy5es PJKH8f2vfE?si=LG53ibaYQI-y7iuC-Tm1nA.

(4) Ibid.

(5) Danielle Lewis (Worship Director), interview with Renee Fisher, Houston, Texas, August 29, 2017.

(6) MetroLyrics, s.v. "Elevation Worship - There is a Cloud Lyrics," accessed on May 10, 2021, https://www.metrolyrics.com/ there-is-a-cloud-lyrics-elevation-worship.html.

(7) Priscilla Shirer, *Awaken: 90 Days with the God who Speaks* (Nashville, TN: B&H Publishing Group, 2001), Day 46.

Chapter 5

(1) *Point Pleasant Register*, s.v. "Genesis 1:14," accessed May 8, 2021, https://www.mydailyregister.com/opinion/44696/search-the-scriptures-a-spiritual-harvest.

(2) *Bible Study Tools*, s.v. "Z@man," accessed June 28, 2017, https://www.biblestudytools.com/lexicons/hebrew/kjv/ zeman.html.

(3) *Bible Study Tools*, s.v. "Chalam," accessed June 28, 2017, http://www.biblestudytools.com/lexicons/hebrew/kjv/cha-lam.html.

(4) Sarah Beth Marr, *Whispers and Wildflowers: 30 Days to Slow Your Pace, Savor Scripture & Draw Closer to God* (Grand Rapids, MI: Baker Books, 2019), 103.

Chapter 6

(1) *MetroLyrics*, s.v. "Unspoken - Reason Lyrics," accessed May 24, 2021, https://www.metrolyrics.com/reason-lyrics-unspoken. html.

(2) Ruth Chou Simons, *Beholding and Becoming: The Art of Everyday Worship* (Eugene, OR: Harvest House Publishers, 2019), 207.

(3) Priscilla Shirer, *Gideon - Bible Study Book: Your weakness. God's Strength.* (Nashville, TN: LifeWay Press, 2013), 57.

(4) Adele Ahlberg Calhoun, *Spiritual Disciplines Handbook: Practices That Transform Us Revised and Expanded* (Downers Grove, IL: IVP Books, 2015), 79.

(5) Ibid, 77.

(6) Ibid, 79.

Chapter 7

(1) *The Atlantic*, s.v. "Paul Harvey," accessed May 2021, https://www.theatlantic.com/politics/archive/2013/02/paul-harveys-1978-so-god-made-a-farmer-speech/272816/.

(2) Maria Furlough, *Breaking the Fear Cycle: How to Find Peace for Your Anxious Heart* (Grand Rapids, MI: Revell, 2018), 115.

(3) *MetroLyrics*, s.v. "Housefires - I'll Give Thanks Lyrics," accessed May 25, 2021, https://www.metrolyrics.com/ill-give-thanks-feat-kirby-kaple-live-lyrics-housefires.html.

(4) Melissa Spoelstra, *Jeremiah - Women's Bible Study Participant Book: Daring to Hope in an Unstable World* (Nashville, TN: Abingdon Press, 2014), 80-81.

(5) *Genius*, s.v. "Jonathan Ogden - Slow Down Lyrics," accessed May 24, 2021, https://genius.com/Jonathan-ogden-slow-down-lyrics.

Epilogue

(1) Sinclair B. Ferguson, *The Holy Spirit: Contours of Christian Theology (*Downers Grove, IL: InterVarsity Press, 1996) 255.

(2) *Blue Letter Bible*, s.v. "Yā'ad," accessed April 1, 2020, https://www.blueletterbible.org/lang/lexicon/lexicon.cfm?strongs=H3259&t=KJV.

What's in Season?

(1) Lara Casey, *Cultivate: A Grace-Filled Guide to Growing an Intentional Life* (Nashville, TN: Thomas Nelson, 2017), 9.

Create Your Own Scripture Garden

(1) *Goodreads*, s.v. "Lady Bird Johnson" accessed May 25, 2021, https://www.goodreads.com/quotes/7307247-where-flowers-bloom-so-does-hope.

CPSIA information can be obtained
at www.ICGtesting.com
Printed in the USA
BVHW030805030122
625351BV00004B/120